THE PARANORMAL INVESTIGATOR

DANNY MOSS

First edition published December 2024

ISBN 979-8-301-45168-3

Published by Project Weird
www.projectweird.com

PROJECT 💀 WEIRD

Contents

Introduction

When I first started out, I never imagined that I'd be writing a book about my journey through the paranormal. My story is something I've talked about in bits and pieces over the years on podcasts, interviews, and TV shows, but I've never really shared the full story. This book is my chance to finally put it all down, to give you a real insight not just into Danny Moss, the paranormal investigator, but into Danny Moss, the human being. It's about how I got here, what I've experienced, and how much it takes to do this full time.

There's so much people don't see about the world I work in. Sure, they watch the TV shows and the YouTube episodes, and maybe they come along to the events we organise, but they don't always see the personal side, the challenges, the emotional toll. People are always asking me how I manage it, how I cope with the pressure of working in the paranormal field, and that's something I want to talk about here.

It's not all ghost hunts and haunted objects. It's a lot of hard work, determination, and a fair bit of drama.

I started out as a teenager with no real interest in the paranormal. My first real brush with the paranormal happened when I was 17, and it completely changed my perspective, and from that point on, my path was set. I ended up founding The Haunted Hunts and leading investigations at some of the UK's most notorious haunted locations. It wasn't easy. We struggled at first, but through grit and perseverance, we grew a following.

Of course, there's more to the story. I've had some pretty intense experiences with haunted objects, like the Grace doll, which became a massive part of my career. I'll never forget the investigation at Nantclwyd y Dre in 2017 when the doll seemed to trigger activity and uneasy feelings, affecting not just me but the guests as well. Then in 2018, the same doll flung itself off a chair, which was caught on camera. It's things like that that remind you how unpredictable and, honestly, unsettling this field can be.

But it's not just the paranormal activity that's challenging. The paranormal community itself can be incredibly toxic. People see you on TV and on the internet, and they think they know you, but they don't see the darker side. It's surreal, but that's the reality of putting yourself out there in this field. It's something I want people to understand, and maybe this book can shed some light on the toll it takes.

Despite all the negativity, I've kept going, and my career has taken off. TV shows like 'Paranormal Captured' and 'The Haunted Hunts' have helped me reach a wider audience, and more recently, we've expanded the 'My Haunted Project'. This was a massive step for us - 24/7 surveillance, a unique guest experience, and a focus on real, long-term paranormal research. Of course, that brought a whole new set of challenges.

Looking forward, we've got big plans. There's the expansion of the 'My Haunted Project' into the US with the Samuel Miller Mansion, and we've moved from YouTube to platforms like Amazon Prime, which opens up so many opportunities for long-term storytelling and deeper investigations.

At the end of the day, this book is for the people who've followed me, for those who are curious about what really goes on behind the scenes. I want to share the highs, the lows, and everything in between. This is my story - the truth about the paranormal world and my place in it.

Where it Began

Before I turned 17, I never gave the paranormal a second thought. It simply wasn't on my radar. Growing up in the North West, my life revolved around football, school, and the usual things a kid focuses on. The closest I'd ever come to anything strange happened when I was about seven years old. My family and I were driving home from one of my parents' friends' houses, passing through Ellesmere Port, an industrial town with sprawling factories and the looming presence of Stanlow, the massive oil refinery.

I remember sitting in the back seat, staring out the window as we drove past the glowing lights and towering chimneys. Something caught my eye. It was a weird, pink ball of light floating in the sky above the factories. It was unlike anything I'd ever seen before. For a moment, I remember thinking, "Oh my God, is that a UFO?" The light hung there for what seemed like ages, hovering above the smoke stacks and refinery towers, before it disappeared just as suddenly as it had appeared. It was odd, but at the time, it didn't stick with me for long. I didn't think much more of it after that.

I grew up in Frodsham, a small market town in Cheshire, known for its picturesque countryside and close-knit community. Situated about 16 miles south of Liverpool, it's the kind of place where everyone knows each other. Frodsham's got its own little claim to fame too. Daniel Craig, the actor who became world-famous for playing James Bond, lived there until his early teens, and Gary Barlow, the singer from Take That, was born and raised in the town. But for me, Frodsham was just home - quiet, familiar, and a good place to grow up.

My life revolved around football. Football was everything to me. If you'd told me back then that I'd one day be deeply involved in the paranormal, I wouldn't have believed it for a second. I'd been playing since I was a kid, when I was 11, I had a trial with Stoke City, and by the time I was 15, I'd had trials with Crewe Alexandra. That was the dream, to play professionally, maybe even for Liverpool.

Not long after my Crewe Alexandra trial, everything changed. I had a cruciate ligament injury in my left knee during a match, and just like that, my football dreams were over. I was absolutely devastated. Football had been my entire life up to that point, the thing I worked hardest at and poured all my energy into. Without it, I felt completely lost. The injury left me stuck at home on crutches, unable to do much of anything, not even go to school. Being away from my friends and the normal routine of Helsby High School just made it worse. It was like everything had been taken away at once.

As the weeks dragged on, the frustration started to build, and it wasn't long before I slipped into a bit of a depression. I had no idea what to do with myself anymore. I was angry and bitter about the whole situation, and things spiralled from there. I started acting out, getting into trouble, and pushing against any authority. I almost got kicked out of high school because of it. By my final year, I was only allowed in school three days a week, and just for drama class, which was about the only thing I still felt like doing.

Drama became a kind of lifeline for me. While everything else in my life felt like it was falling apart, I found that I connected with drama. My teacher, Mrs. Cross, was a real turning point. She sat me down one day after class and told me straight up that I had a real talent for acting and that I should seriously think about pursuing it in college. It was the first time since the injury that I felt like there was something else out there for me, something I could focus on beyond football. That conversation changed my whole mindset. Drama became my new outlet.

At 17, during the period where I was transitioning from football to drama, I had my first proper brush with the paranormal. I was at a mate's house, nothing unusual about the place, just an ordinary family home. There wasn't any history of it being haunted, no spooky backstory, nothing like that. We were just sitting in the living room, hanging out like we always did, when we both heard something out in the hallway. It sounded like someone was moving around, maybe even trying to break in. Immediately, we thought it was an intruder.

Naturally, we went to check it out, feeling that nervous energy creep in. But then it took a turn. Instead of noises in the hallway, we heard something completely different - someone running up and down the stairs. Not once, not twice, but seven or eight times, heavy, fast footsteps thudding up and down the staircase. We stood there, completely still, both hearing it as clear as day, but there was no one there. It was one of those moments where you just freeze, and you look at each other with wide eyes, like, "Are we both hearing this?" We searched the house, convinced we had to find an explanation, maybe a family member messing with us or something, but there was no one.

I had never experienced anything remotely like that before. I wasn't into ghosts or anything paranormal at that point, but that moment shook me to the core. It left me completely confused and rattled, and the strangest part was that even though it freaked me out, I couldn't stop thinking about it. It stuck with me. I kept going over it in my head, trying to figure out how something so loud, so unmistakable, could happen with no explanation. That moment sparked something in me, a curiosity, a need to know more.

Following Mrs. Cross' advice, drama became my main focus, now in college. I ended up getting small acting jobs here and there. I did some corporate work, and I played a character who needed legal defence to help train barristers at Manchester University. I did all kinds of stuff, some more embarrassing than others. The one that still gets me is when I played a rapping Santa Claus in a Christmas advert. Every year, it pops up on those "100 Funniest Christmas Ads" shows, which are those TV specials that look back at cheesy or cringeworthy holiday commercials. And every time I see it, I have to cringe watching myself as a hip-hop Santa.

Eventually, I landed a three-episode role on 'Hollyoaks' playing a thug. 'Hollyoaks' was a big deal for me at the time, even though it was just a few episodes. It's one of the UK's longest-running soaps, known for its young cast and bold storylines, so being part of that was a great opportunity.

Despite these acting gigs, the industry was tough. There was constant rejection, and I needed more stability. I ended up working in a local factory, picking shelves of electrical equipment. It was long hours, starting at half five in the morning, and I hated every minute of it. But throughout all of this, that paranormal experience stuck with me.

Around the age of 18, I started researching paranormal phenomena, specifically ghost-related events. I wasn't particularly interested in UFOs or cryptids like Bigfoot – it was all about ghosts for me. That experience I'd had with my mate at 17 was still something we'd often talk about, trying to make sense of it. It just left this burning curiosity in me, a need to understand what we'd experienced. I started diving into books and websites, learning about paranormal investigations and hauntings, and became fascinated by history and haunted locations. The more I read, the more I was inspired to find answers to these unanswered questions relating to hauntings.

At this point, I wasn't just learning about ghosts in the traditional sense – spirits of the dead – but also started exploring the different types of hauntings. There are what some people call intelligent hauntings, where the spirit is believed to interact with the living, responding to questions or requests. Then there are residual hauntings, where it's more like a replay of an event from the past, with no awareness or interaction from the spirit. These concepts became a bit of an obsession for me.

That's also when my sister Becki came into the picture. She's the complete opposite of me in many ways – she's always been into the paranormal, especially witchcraft and witches, though she's probably more sceptical than I am in some areas. Becki's love for history and art naturally pulled her toward the folklore surrounding witches and the darker aspects of history. One place she'd always wanted to visit was Pendle Hill, famous for its connection to the Pendle witch trials of 1612, where ten women were accused of witchcraft and executed. Pendle Hill has a deep-rooted history, not just with the trials but also with reports of hauntings and strange phenomena tied to the area. It was a perfect blend of our shared interest in history and the paranormal.

So, we eventually made that trip to Pendle Hill as a family. I remember the day clearly. We started in

Newchurch-in-Pendle, a small village nestled in the shadow of the hill, with its old church and the so-called "witch's grave" in the churchyard. It was eerie just being there, knowing that this quiet spot was at the heart of one of the most infamous witch trials in English history.

From Newchurch, it's only a short drive to Barley, where most people start their climb to the top of the hill. From the carpark there's a circular route – a a relatively gentle hike of about five miles that winds around the hill. Even back then, before I was deeply involved in the paranormal, I could feel something about the place. It wasn't just the bleak beauty of the moorland or the imposing rise of the hill itself – it was like the whole area held an energy linking it to its past. The Pendle witch trials, with all their fear and injustice, seemed to seep into the land.

Walking up that hill, I couldn't shake the feeling that the ground itself held the echoes of those accused women, their lives destroyed by superstition and hysteria. I wasn't fully aware of it at the time, but that visit to Pendle Hill was my first proper taste of how a place's dark history can leave an energy behind. It was the first step toward realising that the past doesn't just live in books – it lingers in the very places where it unfolded.

At that point, I was still trying to work out what I wanted to do with my life. I was still in college studying drama, trying to carve out a path in acting, but I had a bit of a rebellious streak and kept finding myself in trouble. I'd get kicked out of places for acting up, pushing boundaries, and not really knowing where I fit in. I was hired by an agency and managed to land some acting jobs, but it wasn't enough to rely on. I'd get the odd gig here and there – the small roles on TV or corporate work – but there was no real consistency or guaranteed income.

Meanwhile, I was balancing everything else life threw at me. Relationships, acting jobs, and that typical teenage lad lifestyle. I was out with my mates, going to the pub, having a drink, meeting girls – all the usual distractions that come with being a young guy finding his way. Even though I was caught up in the day-to-day chaos, there was always this part of me that was drawn to the unexplained. I couldn't help but keep researching, looking into different ghost stories, hauntings, and the history behind paranormal phenomena. It wasn't a career, though, not something I could see myself doing full-time – just a fascination that kept growing.

My friends back then weren't really into the paranormal at all. I hung out with a lot of 'lad lads,' the kind of guys who were more interested in football, girls, and drinking. The idea of ghost hunting or talking about the paranormal just wasn't something that fit into our group. It wasn't cool to be into that sort of thing – we'd be talking about the weekend's match or planning nights out at the pub, not haunted locations or spooky experiences. The conversations were all about banter, football rivalries, and which girl someone had met.

But even in the middle of all that, I never really followed the crowd. While we were all having a laugh and living the typical lad lifestyle, I had this quiet fascination with history and the unknown that none of my mates really knew about. It was something I kept to myself, like a secret interest I didn't share with the group.

Unlike many of today's paranormal investigators, I wasn't really influenced by TV shows back then. 'Most Haunted' was huge in the early 2000s, and I'd watched a few episodes, like everyone did. It was the go-to show for anything paranormal at the time, and for a lot of people, it sparked their interest in ghost hunting. Looking back, it's clear that 'Most Haunted' played a massive role in shaping the paranormal scene in the UK. Yvette Fielding and the team visited supposedly haunted locations, getting scared on camera – it inspired a lot of people to start investigating for themselves. But for me, it wasn't something that ever really grabbed my attention. I was more into horror films back then – anything with a dark, spooky atmosphere would catch my attention.

Despite my fascination with the paranormal, I didn't dive straight into the paranormal. In fact, after that trip to Pendle, I didn't do much more with it for a while. Life took over, as it does, but the interest simmered in the background. By the time I was around 21, I started to revisit the idea. By this time I'd passed my driving test and was beginning to venture out to reputedly haunted locations. One of the first places I visited was Marford, a small, picturesque village in North Wales. Marford has an eerie charm, with many of the houses featuring crucifixes or cross-shaped windows built into their design. The local legend claimed that these crosses were meant to ward off the vengeful female spirit who was said to haunt the village.

According to local legend, she was the spirit of Lady Margaret Blackbourne, who was reportedly murdered by her husband George Blackbourne, and now wandered the village, unable to rest. People believed the crosses kept her at bay. There was something about that story – the combination of such an enduring local legend, the documented history, and the physical symbols in the architecture that last to this day. It wasn't just about ghost stories anymore, it was about the connection between history, place, and the unexplained.

At the same time, I was struggling on with my acting career. I had a few massive auditions that felt like they could be career-defining moments. One was for a BBC drama, which I actually got a callback for, and another was for 'Emmerdale', where I auditioned for the role of

Ross Barton. For anyone unfamiliar, 'Emmerdale' is one of the UK's longest-running and most popular soap operas, set in the Yorkshire Dales. Landing a role on a show like that would have been life-changing – a regular part in a series with a huge following. Ross Barton ended up being a big character in 'Emmerdale', appearing for over five years. It was the kind of role that would have really propelled my acting career, but, as is often the case in the acting world, the part went to someone else – in this case, Michael Parr.

That's the thing about acting: sometimes you miss out on roles for reasons you'll never know, and it can be down to something as simple as the way you look or how tall you are. You can nail the audition, but someone else just fits the character in the casting director's mind a little bit better. It's a tough industry, full of highs and lows, and after a while, the rejections start to weigh you down. I did land some parts I didn't think I'd get, but the ones I really thought I had in the bag seemed to slip through my fingers. It was disheartening.

By this point, I'd ditched the warehouse job, and I was working behind the bar at a local golf club, and I really didn't enjoy this job either. It was just a way to get by while waiting for that big break, but it never came. The reality of the acting world hit hard, and I started questioning whether it was something I could keep pursuing. I was stuck in this limbo – chasing a dream while also trying to figure out how to pay the bills. It wasn't an easy place to be.

That was when I started to really reconsider my path. My interest in the paranormal had been growing steadily, and it just kept pulling me in. At the time, stepping away from acting and moving into ghost hunting felt like a strange move. Acting was something I'd spent years working towards. But there was this constant feeling that I needed to explore haunted locations, go on adventures, and see what was out there. It wasn't just a passing interest, it was something that gripped me. I wasn't sure how or what that would look like back then – whether it could be a career or just a side hobby – but I knew I had to give it a go.

The Haunted Hunts

With my decision made, I knew it was time to immerse myself in the paranormal world. The first step on this journey was attending organised ghost-hunting events, where members of the public could experience haunted locations firsthand. These events were few and far between back then, but were designed for people like me – curious, sceptical, and searching for answers. Guided by a team of investigators equipped with gadgets that promised to detect paranormal activity, these nights offered an opportunity to learn the ropes. It was my first real introduction to the structured side of ghost hunting, and it didn't take long for me to realise that the paranormal world attracted all sorts of people.

There were believers who seemed to see ghosts in every flicker of light or cold draught, and that made it challenging for someone like me, who approached things with a healthy dose of scepticism. Listening to claims of "feeling energies" or hearing whispers in the air left me questioning how much of it was real and how much was just wishful thinking. Still, these events were valuable. They gave me a glimpse into how other investigators worked and whether their methods matched the expectations I was forming. Some of it did, but much of it felt overly dramatic, almost as though people were desperate to find something that might not be there.

The place that really piqued my interest was Plas Teg, a Grade I listed Jacobean house in North Wales, which I visited during one of these paranormal events. Plas Teg had a reputation for being one of the most haunted locations in the area, and it didn't take long for me to be drawn in by its eerie atmosphere and rich history. It was during this investigation that I started experimenting and trying things that others weren't doing at the time. A lot of people were heavily into methods like Ouija boards, table tipping, and mediumship. These were the staple techniques used on public ghost hunts. But that approach didn't sit right with me. I'd seen these methods being used on events, and they felt too subjective, too reliant on belief.

I wanted to take a different route. Instead of trying to communicate with spirits through these traditional means, I focused on setting up cameras, covering every angle of the rooms, and then just waiting to see if anything happened. I moved away from the spiritual and subjective side of things, wanting instead to capture hard, physical evidence. For me, the idea was simple: if there was something paranormal out there, I wanted to catch it on film. I want undeniable proof that couldn't be dismissed or misinterpreted. Plas Teg gave me the chance to start applying that more investigative approach, and I felt like I was finally heading in a direction that made sense to me.

One of the moments that really stuck with me happened during my second visit to Plas Teg. We were in a room that felt typically still, the kind of atmosphere you'd expect in an old house like that, and thick with history. Suddenly, the heavy wooden door to the room opened by itself. At first, my logical side kicked in. I immediately thought it must have been a draught, or maybe someone was coming into the room from the other side. The door opened so deliberately and quickly that we all expected someone to walk in right after it. But when no one appeared, it made me pause. This wasn't just any flimsy door, either - it was one of those heavy, solid doors you find in these old properties, the kind that doesn't just swing open on its own. It didn't creak open slowly, like a typical draught might cause. It moved in a way that didn't feel natural.

That moment really made me think. It wasn't just a random creak or noise that could be easily dismissed. It reminded me of the footsteps I heard when I was 17. It was the same kind of unexplainable occurrence that throws your whole sense of reality off balance. It was another significant moment for me, something that deepened my interest in the paranormal and made me wonder if there really was something more to all of this.

From that point on, I started to take things more seriously. I was at Plas Teg so often that I became friends with the people who ran it, and my time there wasn't just about casual visits anymore. I was really delving into the experiences I was having. I had more strange occurrences there, moments that made me question everything I thought I knew about the paranormal. It was a gradual process, but I found myself getting more and more drawn into the idea that the history of these places might hold the key to understanding the strange things I was witnessing. I started researching who could be haunting the location, piecing together the historical context, trying to find a link between the past and the present phenomena.

At the same time, my acting career was still at a standstill, and my job behind the bar at the golf club was miserable. The lack of fulfilment was draining me, and I knew I couldn't keep doing it. The idea of hosting paranormal events started to seem like a way out. I had seen how these events worked, and with my growing obsession for the paranormal, it felt like something I could turn into a career. I wasn't sure how to go about it at first, but I'd seen other people running similar events, and I thought, "Why not me?" It was a chance to combine my love for investigating haunted locations with something that could actually get me out of a dead-end job. This was the start of a new chapter, a way to turn my passion into something real.

At that point, I started learning the tricks of the trade. I watched a lot of shows like 'Ghost Hunters International' and followed the T.A.P.S. team (The Atlantic Paranormal Society), which was led by Jason Hawes and Grant Wilson. The show had a huge impact on the paranormal field in the early 2000s. I was particularly drawn to their methodical approach, how they'd go into these large, often historic locations, set up a range of cameras and equipment, and try to find rational explanations for what was happening. Unlike other shows that leaned heavily into the spooky or dramatic, 'Ghost Hunters International' and its US counterpart had a more grounded feel. They didn't just jump to conclusions, they'd interview the owners, look into the history of the place, and actually try to debunk claims before deciding if something paranormal was going on.

I knew not to take everything on TV as gospel. There's always an element of entertainment when you're dealing with TV shows, but seeing the T.A.P.S. team capture things on camera and hearing the stories from the people they interviewed was hard to ignore. It got me thinking. I'd already had my own experiences that I couldn't explain, like the door at Plas Teg or the footsteps years earlier, and those moments kept pushing me to question things. Maybe hauntings were real, and I wanted to find out for myself. If there was even a chance that these things were genuinely happening, I needed to be the one investigating them.

My sister, Becki, played a big role in this too. Her interest in the paranormal made her a great sounding board for my ideas. We'd have long conversations about how to approach investigations in a way that felt more grounded, more scientific. I didn't want to create an events company that relied on things like Ouija boards or table tipping, methods that I felt were too subjective and often led by people's expectations.

Instead, I wanted to focus on using technology, cameras, gadgets, and equipment that could capture real evidence, if there was any to be found. The idea was to create events that would attract people who were more like me: curious but not fully convinced. These would be people who were 50/50 about the paranormal - not blind believers, but open-minded sceptics, ready to see if there was any truth behind the stories. It felt like a fresh approach, something that could give people a new way of experiencing the paranormal without relying on old-school methods that felt more like superstition than investigation.

At that time, I was experimenting with gadgets, though I didn't always use them correctly. One of the first things I brought into the field was cat balls, those little pet toys that light up when they're moved. I remember seeing them in a pet shop and thinking they'd be perfect for detecting movement during paranormal investigations. At the time, I hadn't seen anyone use them before, and they worked well in some situations, giving a visual cue when something moved them. Along with that, I used electromagnetic field (EMF) meters, thinking they could detect ghosts. In reality, EMF meters are designed to measure spikes in electromagnetic energy, which can sometimes explain away strange occurrences like flickering lights, electrical interference, or even odd feelings or sensations. But back then, I didn't fully understand their proper use.

I also experimented with temperature guns, believing I could track down cold spots, a common sign people associate with hauntings. What I didn't realise then was that these tools measure surface temperatures, not the air around you, so I wasn't really getting the kind of data I needed for a paranormal investigation.

Despite using these gadgets, I quickly realised that rather than relying on gadgets that overpromise and underdeliver, the most reliable tools were still voice recorders and cameras. If you can capture a disembodied voice or strange movement on camera and prove there was no one else in the room, then you've got something solid. Even back then, those were the devices that gave me the most compelling results.

For me, cameras are the cornerstone of any investigation. Documenting visual phenomena is crucial, and I always make sure to set up high-quality cameras in key spots. In dark or low-light locations, infrared or night-vision cameras can be used to capture visual evidence without ruining the ambiance of an event by using bright camera lights.

Alongside cameras, good audio recorders are indispensable. Strange sounds or disembodied voices are common during investigations, and capturing those with clarity is vital. I often spread recorders across different parts of a location to maximise coverage, and a good microphone can pick up sounds that the human ear might miss.

I've also used motion detectors in the past, though I've learnt not to rely on them too heavily. They can still be effective when used strategically, but it's important to back up their results with other forms of evidence. Over time, I've learnt that simplicity is key. Many gadgets give false readings, especially in environments with fluctuating electrical currents or other interference, and they can end up distracting from the investigation itself. Now, I focus on the tools that provide clear, objective data. It's not about having loads of gadgets, it's about using the right ones in the right way. That's a lesson that's stuck with me throughout my journey into the paranormal.

When I first started running paranormal events, I didn't really give much thought to the issue of making money from it. These days, there's a lot of criticism from certain groups about people "cashing in" on the paranormal, as if making a living from something you're passionate about is a negative thing. But back then, in 2012, social media wasn't as big a part of our lives as it is now, and the kind of public scrutiny we see today didn't exist.

I think it's important to highlight that there's nothing wrong with turning your passion into a career. People profit from their interests in all kinds of fields, whether it's history, archaeology, or even sports. But for some reason, when it comes to the paranormal, there's a stigma attached to it. Some people assume that if you're making money from it, then your intentions aren't genuine or that you're somehow exploiting the field. To me, that's misguided. Yes, there are people out there who might take advantage of others' beliefs for personal gain, but most of us are in this because we're genuinely fascinated by the unknown.

My mindset was simple: I loved paranormal investigating, and I wanted to share that passion with others and do it in my own way. I'd had some incredible experiences, and I wanted people to feel that same excitement and curiosity. If I could make some money along the way, that was just a bonus, not the driving force.

So, in 2012, I set up my events company, though I had no idea at the time how I was going to make it work. The only thing I knew for sure was that I had to sell enough tickets for events to cover the cost of hiring locations, and money was tight. I didn't have the luxury of throwing cash at advertising or fancy websites, so I had to figure out a way to get people to find my company. I started thinking about how people actually search for ghost hunting events online. Most would type something like "ghost hunts" or "haunted hunts" into Google, so I concluded that's how I'd get discovered. I kept it simple and named the company The Haunted Hunts, purely with that in mind - making it easier for people to find me.

I didn't overthink it at the time, and honestly, the name did the job. It was straightforward and did exactly what I needed it to do: get people to click on it when they were searching for ghost hunts. It worked, but not immediately. I started getting enquiries soon after setting up the site, but it was a slow start. A few clicks here and there eventually turned into bookings.

In hindsight, I'm not as keen on the name now. It's not uncommon for people to swap out the word "hunts" for an unfortunate rhyming word, and I've had more jokes made about that than I can count. But at the time, it wasn't really something I thought about. The name served its purpose, and in the early days, that was all that mattered, getting people through the door.

We ran our first events at The Old Hall Hotel, an atmospheric building in my hometown with an incredible haunted history. Originally, it was two 17th-century cottages that were later merged and transformed into what became known as The White House in the 19th century, before its eventual conversion into a hotel. The place had a real presence, and the stories from staff about paranormal activity were enough to convince me it would be the perfect location to start. One of the chefs had witnessed some truly bizarre things, and the building's layout, with its old-world charm, really added to the feel of the investigations. The events started with me, Becki, and a small team. I remember our first event, only about six people showed up. It wasn't the biggest of launches, but the energy of the place made it feel like we were onto something special.

In addition to The Old Hall, we also hosted events at Ye Olde King's Head, which is now My Haunted Hotel in Chester. But my first attempt at running an event there didn't exactly go to plan. I had to cancel because I didn't make enough money to cover the deposit. That was a tough moment, one of those points where you start to question everything. I'd already paid for the website, photos, public liability insurance, and refreshments, all the essentials. But when the bookings didn't come through, I had this sinking feeling that maybe it wasn't going to work.

Fortunately, it didn't put me off. Alongside The Old Hall and Ye Olde King's Head, I added two more locations to the roster: Stanley Palace in Chester, with its striking Jacobean architecture and long-standing reputation for hauntings, and Pen-y-Lan Hall, a grand Tudor-Gothic country house in North Wales. Pen-y-Lan was especially atmospheric, tucked away in the countryside with an eerie, isolated feel that made it perfect for ghost hunts.

These four locations were the foundation of my early events, each offering a different kind of experience that helped shape what The Haunted Hunts would eventually become... if only I could get guests on the events. It was a slow start, and ticket sales were low. I genuinely worried that I'd made a huge mistake.

The turning point came when I started advertising the events on Facebook buy-and-sell groups. These are local community groups, like "Cheshire Buy and Sell" or "Chester for Sale," where people post items for sale or promote services. I thought it was worth a shot, so I listed my events there, and to my surprise, I got far more interest than I ever had by just sharing on my personal Facebook or in the few paranormal groups that existed at the time. Back then, there weren't nearly as many paranormal groups online as there are today, so the buy-and-sell sites worked far better for reaching a local audience.

Looking back, I think one of the main reasons the events didn't sell initially was because, in 2012 and 2013, ghost hunting events weren't as popular or widely known, at least not in the UK. Most people didn't even realise it was an option to spend a weekend night exploring haunted locations. The paranormal events field was much smaller back then and nowhere near as oversaturated as it is today. It wasn't that people weren't interested in the paranormal, they just didn't know these kinds of experiences were available to them.

Things gradually started to pick up with the events, particularly at Stanley Palace and Pen-y-Lan Hall. I wasn't making a fortune, but I was seeing a small profit – maybe a couple of hundred quid per night after covering all the costs. It was enough to pay for the location hire and give me a bit of extra spending money. It felt like progress, but it wasn't enough to rely on full-time. I still had to keep my part-time job at the golf club, working three or four shifts a week just to make ends meet. Balancing both the events and the job was tough, but I was determined to keep pushing forward.

At first, some of the events attracted an odd mix of characters, people claiming to be mediums or those who'd act possessed during the night. But as the company grew, the crowd shifted to what I'd call a more "normal" demographic. We began to draw in couples where one partner would be the sceptic, dragged along reluctantly. By the end of the night, they'd often turn to me and say, "I've really enjoyed this. You've made me curious about something I never thought I'd be interested in." Then there were groups of girls coming along for the thrill of the ghost hunt, not hardcore believers but looking for an exciting, memorable night out. These were exactly the kind of people I wanted to attract – those who weren't fully sold on the paranormal but were open to experiencing something different.

As the events gained traction, I started noticing something that felt like a real turning point: we were building a regular customer base. People were coming back to multiple events, and that was a huge moment for me. It made me realise that we were doing something right and that what we offered stood out. Our approach was rational and realistic, and I think people appreciated that. I wasn't trying to sell a guaranteed ghostly encounter. I'd always be upfront, telling people, "Look, if nothing happens tonight, it could end up being a long and boring evening, but it'll still be an experience." That honesty struck a chord.

To meet demand, we expanded our events to more prominent and historically significant locations. One of these was Tudor World in Stratford-upon-Avon, a living history museum located in the heart of the town, close to the Royal Shakespeare Company. The museum captures the atmosphere of Tudor England, and with its long-standing history and authentic setting, it has long been associated with ghost stories. The building itself dates back to the 16th century, making it the perfect backdrop for paranormal investigations. It had even been featured on the popular TV show 'Most Haunted', which only added to its reputation as one of the most haunted places in Stratford.

We also added places like Ruthin Gaol in Wales, a former Victorian prison that had seen its share of dark history, and Tatton Old Hall in Cheshire, an Elizabethan building that eventually became our main base for a time. The hall, with its creaking floors and centuries of history, was perfect for our regular events. Hosting there gave us a permanent spot for The Haunted Hunts and cemented it as a go-to location for ghost hunting in the area.

Additionally, we branched out to other well-known haunted sites such as Ordsall Hall in Manchester, a grand manor with a long history of ghost sightings, and Newsham Park Hospital in Liverpool, a former orphanage and mental asylum that had developed a fearsome reputation for intense paranormal activity. These larger locations allowed us to increase our event sizes, accommodating up to 30 people. By 2016, the company had gained real momentum, and these haunted locations became the core of our success.

One of the standout locations for me was Stanley Palace in Chester. We kept hearing strange footsteps there, which became a regular occurrence during our investigations. That's when I really started delving into data analysis, measuring times, and trying to understand patterns in paranormal activity. I wasn't just looking for a fleeting moment of unexplained phenomena – I wanted to figure out why it was happening, how it was happening, and whether we could replicate it.

To make sure we had solid evidence, I began documenting everything methodically. We would keep continuous logs of audio and video recordings, making sure to label each file with the exact time and location. Post-investigation review became a crucial part of the process, as I took time to go through everything we captured, ruling out natural causes before even considering the paranormal. This approach gave our investigations more credibility and helped us dig deeper into the unexplained phenomena we were experiencing at Stanley Palace.

Of course, there were difficult moments too. Not every night was a success, and there were times when guests would leave disappointed, especially if they'd come with high expectations. People often arrived with the belief that something paranormal would happen within the first ten minutes, influenced by the fast-paced drama of ghost hunting TV shows.

In reality, many nights passed quietly, with nothing out of the ordinary occurring, and those nights could feel like pulling teeth. Managing the guests' expectations was a constant challenge. But even on those quieter nights, we always tried to leave them with something. We'd ask, "Have you learnt any new techniques? Did you enjoy exploring the history of the building?" Even if the paranormal eluded us, we wanted them to walk away with a richer experience, whether it was an appreciation for the location's past or a deeper understanding of the investigative process. It was all part of building The Haunted Hunts name. And while the events were steadily growing in popularity, bigger opportunities lay just around the corner, ones that would take me in directions I hadn't yet anticipated.

Search for the Truth

In 2017, everything changed for me. The Haunted Hunts had been running strong for a few years, steadily building momentum. But in the last 18 months, something had shifted. There was a noticeable spike in interest around paranormal events. It wasn't just a slow, steady growth, it felt like the entire genre was booming. More and more events companies were cropping up across the UK, and ghost hunting TV shows were becoming more mainstream. The paranormal had always had a niche following, but now it was moving closer to the public eye.

This rise in interest probably coincided with the fact that I was becoming more deeply involved in the field myself. I started connecting with other investigators, attending more events, and forming networks with people like Paul Stevenson and Andy Soar from Haunted Magazine. I was also engaging with Facebook groups that were dedicated to the paranormal, learning from others and sharing my own experiences. The more I connected with people in the field, the more I could see how much the genre was growing.

The Haunted Hunts was fulfilling, and it had been doing very well, but I felt ready to take things further. I wasn't content with just hosting events anymore. I wanted to explore new possibilities and make a bigger impact in the paranormal field.

That's when I made the decision to use my background in acting and my experience in front of a camera to create my own ghost hunting show. It wasn't a spur-of-the-moment idea, I knew exactly what I wanted to achieve. I didn't want just any ghost show. I wanted something that reflected my beliefs and the approach I'd taken with The Haunted Hunts. I wanted to explore haunted locations with honesty, seeking the truth behind the activity, rather than relying on sensationalism or gimmicks.

So, I reached out to a local production company called LT Media. They weren't known for television, but they had a good reputation for filming events and working with local businesses. It seemed like the right place to start, and I was confident that, with the right team, this could be the next big step in my journey.

We called the show 'Search for the Truth', which felt perfect. I didn't want a typical ghost hunting title. The concept was straightforward: it would be a paranormal series focused on searching for the truth behind haunted locations without sensationalising the events.

We filmed the pilot in the offices above LT Media. A pilot is essentially the first episode or a test version of a TV show, used to showcase the concept and prove its viability to networks or potential backers. We were fortunate enough to have a talented graphic designer on board who had previously worked on some major TV projects, including creating a CGI dragon for 'Game of Thrones'. He helped design the show's opening credits and even put together a 3D walkthrough of our featured locations. It was a lucky find, and as things came together, it started to feel like the show was really becoming a reality.

At that point, I had no clue how to operate a camera or produce anything. I was just the guy who would host the show and present it, but I knew I needed to build a capable team around me to make it work. The first person I brought on board was Becki. She had a solid background in the film and television industry, having worked behind the scenes as a costume designer. She'd studied film and TV at York University and had gained hands-on experience on various sets, so she knew the ropes when it came to production. Becki also brought balance to the project, she was creative but always carried a healthy level of scepticism. She wasn't just someone who could help with the technical side. Becki had been with me throughout my paranormal journey from the start. Her input was invaluable because she could question things and push for rational explanations. There was no way I could move forward with this project without her.

Next, we brought in Sian, one of our paranormal investigators who had been with The Haunted Hunts on events for about 18 months. Sian had a solid understanding of the paranormal and brought both knowledge and experience to the team. She had been on countless investigations and knew what to expect, which made her a natural fit for the show. Finally, we needed someone who could handle all the tech, which was a vital part of any paranormal investigation. We put out an ad and found Connor. He turned out to be the perfect fit, not only because he had extensive knowledge of the equipment we wanted to use, like motion sensors and EMF detectors, but also because he looked the part. With his glasses and gadget-heavy persona, Connor was a classic techie. He fit into the team seamlessly and, unexpectedly, ended up being deeply involved in the research aspect of the show too, helping us understand the technology behind each piece of equipment and contributing to the investigations in ways we hadn't initially planned.

Once we had shot the pilot, the next step was pitching the show to various TV channels. We put together a strong pitching deck - a comprehensive presentation that laid out the entire format of the episodes, explained the concept behind the show, and clearly stated what we wanted to achieve with 'Search for the Truth'. The pilot was the key part of this, showcasing exactly how we intended to approach paranormal investigations with a focus on evidence and historical context. Despite how solid it felt to us, the pitching process wasn't easy. To be honest, we had very little interest from anyone at first. TV is a competitive world, and trying to break into it with a paranormal show, especially one that didn't fit the usual sensationalist mould, was tough. There were days when it felt like we'd never get a break. But after weeks of persistence, I finally managed to land a meeting with Made Television in Liverpool. It felt like a glimmer of hope in what had been a pretty discouraging process.

Made Television was a network that operated local TV stations across the UK, including Made in Liverpool. Their main focus was on local content, but they would occasionally share shows across their wider network, which included stations in cities like Bristol, Cardiff, and Leeds. When Made in Liverpool accepted 'Search for the Truth', it was a huge moment. I didn't want it to be limited to just one area, though, so I pushed hard for it to air across the entire Made TV network. Thankfully, they agreed, and suddenly we had a national platform. It felt incredible. Here we were, with a six-episode series airing on Sunday nights around 7pm, a prime-time slot that we couldn't have asked for a better placement in. The first episode brought in around 234,000 viewers, which blew us away. By the end of the series, viewership had steadily grown, and we peaked at around 800,000. For a locally produced paranormal show, those numbers were massive, and it felt like a real breakthrough.

The series featured some familiar locations from my early events, such as Ye Olde King's Head, Pen-y-Lan Hall, and Stanley Palace. We also branched out into new locations like Mill Street Barracks and Whittington Castle. Mill Street Barracks in St Helens, with its history as a military base, was reputed to have housed ghostly soldiers, making it another prime spot for investigation. Whittington Castle, a picturesque medieval fortress in Shropshire, brought its own chilling tales of hauntings and apparitions. Each episode followed us as we investigated these haunted sites, searching for answers.

At that time, I felt like I'd really made it. I was in a good place in my life, both personally and professionally. After some tough teenage years and a rocky start to adulthood, I'd finally started to find my footing. The reckless behaviour of my youth was behind me, and I was getting my head on straight. Financially, I was more stable than I'd ever been, thanks to both The Haunted Hunts events and 'Search for the Truth'.

At 27 years old, I was maturing into the person I wanted to be. I'd managed to build a TV show from scratch with my own vision and a dedicated team. I was doing something I genuinely loved, exploring the paranormal and sharing those experiences with others. It was a moment where everything seemed to click, and for the first time in a long time, I was genuinely happy and proud of what I'd achieved.

By putting my paranormal passion out there on TV, I started getting more feedback from friends and family. A lot of my mates were really supportive, although they'd still take the piss from time to time, which was expected in our group. It was all in good humour, and deep down, they were behind me and proud of what I was achieving.

My relationships with my family, which had been strained in the past, were improving, and I was growing closer to them again. My family, while supportive, were naturally more sceptical about the whole paranormal side of things. They weren't sure where it was all heading, but they respected the fact that I was doing something I was passionate about and that it was paying off.

What surprised me most was the level of recognition I started to get. People would see me out and say things like, "You're doing great, smashing it on TV." It was surreal at first to go from working a regular job to being recognised for something I loved. I wasn't expecting that kind of attention, but it was a good feeling. It was one of those times when everything seemed to be falling into place, and I was enjoying the ride.

Unfortunately, we only made one series of 'Search for the Truth'. Despite its success and strong viewer numbers, we couldn't secure a second season. The channel was bought out, and the new owners shifted their focus away from the kind of content we were producing. Not long after, the entire network folded, and just like that, the show was over. I was disappointed, but I wasn't ready to give up. What I didn't know then was that my journey was about to take a darker turn, because that's when I met Grace.

The Grace Doll

While we were still waiting to hear back about the ultimately rejected commission for a second series of 'Search for the Truth', something far stranger began to take hold. The Grace doll saga, as it would come to be known, quickly became one of the most bizarre and unsettling experiences of my entire paranormal career.

Dolls have been beloved playthings for children for thousands of years, with their history dating back as far as 2000 BC. Yet in recent years, they've taken on a different kind of fascination. While young children continue to see dolls as sources of comfort and fun, for some adults in the paranormal community, dolls have become a subject of unease. Stories of haunted or cursed dolls have been making headlines, and more people are now buying and selling so-called haunted dolls on sites like eBay.

This shift in perception isn't entirely random. According to Linda Rodriguez McRobbie, who wrote about the topic for 'Smithsonian Magazine', the fear of dolls really began in the 19th century, when advances in toy-making made them more realistic. Dolls began to have human-like skin, glass eyes that seemed to follow you, and even mechanical parts that allowed them to blink or speak. While these innovations made dolls more lifelike, they also crossed into the realm of the uncanny, triggering something deep within us that finds comfort in the familiar but unease in something that's almost, but not quite, human.

This phenomenon is known as the "uncanny valley," a term coined by Japanese robotics engineer Masahiro Mori in 1970. It describes the discomfort people feel when something appears human but is clearly inanimate, and it's part of what makes some dolls feel unsettling. Interestingly, children don't seem to experience this discomfort until about the age of nine, when they begin to develop the instinct to judge whether something has a mind of its own.

This anxiety around dolls has been magnified by their portrayal in horror films and stories, where they're often depicted as vessels for evil. It's a theme that first came to prominence in 1963, when 'The Twilight Zone' aired the now-famous 'Living Doll' episode. In it, a girl's doll, Talky Tina, begins as a sweet companion but soon turns threatening, even saying, "I'm going to kill you."

Dolls took on a more terrifying persona in the late 1980s with 'Child's Play' and the introduction of Chucky, a murderous doll possessed by a serial killer's spirit. More recently, the Annabelle doll from 'The Conjuring' series has left her mark on horror fans, particularly chilling because her story is rooted in a real-life paranormal case.

Now, let me be clear: when it came to the idea of haunted dolls, I am a sceptic through and through. Haunted items had never been on my radar. If anyone had mentioned the idea of a doll being haunted, I'd have been the first to dismiss it as nonsense. But everything shifted when Grace came into the picture. Grace was a doll with no known history, no eerie backstory, and no prior claims of paranormal activity. She was just an ordinary china doll, likely from the 1980s or 1990s. Or so I thought...

We had been using Grace for about three or four years at that point as a trigger object for The Haunted Hunts events. In paranormal investigations, a trigger object is a familiar item that's placed in a location with the hope that spirits or entities might interact with it. The idea is to offer something that holds significance to the alleged spirits. For instance, in a jail, you might place a set of old keys on a table, hoping that a former inmate might attempt to move them. If you're investigating a location said to be haunted by children, you'd often use toys or dolls, items that might appeal to child spirits.

Grace fit this role perfectly, but she was always just a tool, nothing more. We never treated her as anything special, never thought she held any paranormal significance beyond being a potential prompt for spirit interaction. She was just an object that blended into the background of our investigations, one of many we used to try and get a reaction from whatever might be present. At that point, we never thought twice about her.

In October 2017, we hosted an investigation at a historic building in North Wales called Nantclwyd y Dre. It's a Grade I listed house, known for being the oldest timbered townhouse in Wales, with sections of the structure dating back to the 15th century. The house has a deep and complex history, having survived significant moments like the burning of Ruthin during the rebellion led by Owain Glyndŵr in 1400 against English rule.

Nantclwyd y Dre also has a reputation for being one of the most haunted locations in Wales. Many who visit report strange occurrences, from inexplicable footsteps to shadowy figures glimpsed in the halls. It's the sort of place that naturally carries an eerie, heavy atmosphere. That night, we were prepared for some odd happenings, but what I wasn't prepared for was what happened next. It would be a turning point in how I viewed haunted objects, and Grace in particular.

Up until that night, I had never encountered anything truly disturbing during my years of paranormal investigations. I was always fascinated by the history of these places, but nothing had ever felt particularly threatening. That all changed on this night at Nantclwyd y Dre.

Out of nowhere, multiple guests reported strange physical sensations, and things started to spiral out of control. What made it even more alarming was that this wasn't isolated to one group. Different groups, who had no contact with each other, were all describing the same symptoms: a burning sensation in their eyes, sharp pains in the palms of their hands and the soles of their feet, and intense headaches. Even I felt it, and I'd never experienced anything remotely like that before. The atmosphere shifted, and at one point, one of the female guests became so overwhelmed that she broke down completely. We ended up having to carry her out of the building, something I'd never had to do at any event before. It was unnerving, to say the least.

Throughout the night, we kept hearing a strange and unsettling pattern of three knocks. We did everything we could to track down the source. We checked doors, windows, and floorboards, but no matter how hard we tried, we couldn't explain it. As always, we approached it with scepticism, trying to debunk any possible causes, but this was happening all over the building, in different rooms and at different times. There was no obvious explanation, and that only made it more unnerving. By the end of the night, I was left genuinely shaken. It felt like something beyond what I was prepared for.

We returned to Nantclwyd y Dre six months later, this time bringing the Grace doll along as a trigger object. We set her up in a room known as the school room, placing her on the back of a chair. Many of the same guests who had attended the October event came back for this one, eager to see if the strange activity would repeat. Sure enough, the unsettling pattern of three knocks began again, echoing through the building, and several people reported experiencing the same physical symptoms of burning sensations, sharp pains, and headaches.

Then something happened that I still can't fully explain. Grace, who had been sitting securely on the back of the chair, suddenly flung herself forward, as if something had physically moved her. The way she was positioned made it impossible for her to simply topple over on her own, it wasn't a case of her slipping or tipping. She literally somersaulted off the chair in a way that defied all logic and gravity. To this day, that moment still baffles me, and it marked the beginning of something much darker with Grace.

Toward the end of the investigation, a group of about 12 people, including myself, were gathered in a room when something truly bizarre occurred. A crucifix, which had been firmly fixed to a door, suddenly came loose and swung down, ending up in an inverted position. It didn't fall off completely - it was still attached to the door by its lower fixing, but now it was hanging upside down. That disturbed me more than anything I had ever experienced before.

An inverted crucifix has long been associated with anti-Christian symbolism, sometimes even linked to satanic imagery in popular culture. While it can traditionally represent St. Peter's crucifixion, which is more benign, in paranormal circles, it's often seen as a sinister sign. Seeing that cross hanging upside down in the middle of a paranormal investigation shook me deeply. It was as if something was trying to send a message, and that moment left a lasting impression on everyone in the room.

To make things even stranger, one of the guests that night was wearing a crucifix necklace, and we all stood in shock as we watched it rise off her neck. The chain seemed to strain under an invisible force, and then, to everyone's amazement, it snapped, and the crucifix came off entirely. The whole thing took about three or four seconds to unfold, and all 12 of us witnessed it at the same time. There was no one near her, no obvious cause, just this surreal moment that left us all stunned.

I had never seen anything like it in my life. It wasn't just the inexplicable movement of the necklace, it was the fact that we all saw it happen, right in front of our eyes. That was the moment everything shifted for me. The paranormal wasn't just something I was trying to prove or understand anymore - it had become undeniably real. I had witnessed something that science simply couldn't explain, and that experience changed everything.

We all went home after that event, still reeling from the bizarre occurrences and trying to process everything. But the strangeness didn't end at Nantclwyd y Dre. Over the next three days, things took an even weirder turn. We had an office where we worked on production, and after the investigation, we left the Grace doll there. At first, nothing seemed out of the ordinary, but soon, we began to notice strange, subtle movements from the doll. It wasn't something we were actively watching for, but small changes in her position started to catch our attention, things like the angle of her head or the placement of her arms.

By the third day, I was getting more suspicious. There had to be a rational explanation, but I couldn't shake the feeling that something was off. To test it, I drew a chalk outline around the doll before leaving the office that evening, making sure she was in a fixed position. I then locked up the office securely, knowing no one could get in. The next morning, I was the first to return, and to my surprise, Grace had moved outside of the chalk line. There was no logical explanation. No one had been in the office, and yet the doll had shifted.

That was the moment I knew something wasn't right, and it wasn't just a coincidence.

What followed were months of increasingly unsettling events centred around Grace, and it completely shook me to my core. For years, I had approached the paranormal with a sceptic's mindset, always looking for logical explanations and rationalising strange occurrences. But after everything we had witnessed with Grace, I couldn't deny what I had seen. The constant activity surrounding the doll was too much to ignore. It wasn't just the odd incident here or there, it was a pattern of events that defied explanation.

The whole Grace doll incident had shaken me to my core, and I honestly didn't know what to do with it. I was genuinely freaked out by what had happened. To distance myself from the doll and get it out of my sight, I decided to store it in the basement of Stanley Palace in Chester, where we were still holding paranormal events. I didn't tell many people about it, only the caretaker knew that I had put Grace down there. Then, something even stranger happened. Janet, the secretary of Stanley Palace, told me she had been hearing a woman screaming coming from the basement. The eerie part was that she had no idea I had hidden the doll down there, and the caretaker hadn't mentioned it to her either. When I heard that, I felt an immediate sense of unease. What was going on? Why was Grace still causing chaos even after I'd tried to get rid of her? It felt like whatever this was, it wasn't done with me yet.

My team and I conducted several investigations around Grace at Stanley Palace, and no matter where we placed her, we kept hearing the same three knocks that had haunted us back at Nantclwyd y Dre. It was uncanny how consistent the phenomenon was, almost as if it followed the doll. The knocks would happen at different times, in different parts of the building, but always in that distinct pattern. I'd never found claims of haunted objects to be very credible before, thinking they were more of a gimmick or a way to sensationalise paranormal activity. But Grace was starting to challenge everything I believed. It was becoming increasingly difficult to dismiss the possibility that this ordinary-looking doll might be harbouring something far from ordinary.

At this point, I started doing something completely out of character, I began investing in and collecting so-called haunted artefacts. It wasn't just about Grace anymore. My curiosity had been sparked, and I wanted to see if other objects could carry the same kind of strange energy.

One of the first things I bought was a chest from an antique shop. It was an old, weathered wooden chest that looked like it came straight from the 19th century, like something you'd imagine a pirate would use to store treasure. The shop owner had told me some strange stories about the chest. He'd captured bizarre footage on his CCTV of swirling lights that moved erratically around it. It wasn't the usual dust particles or insects you'd expect to see on camera, this was something different, something that stood out.

The chest also had a peculiar marking carved into it, an unusual symbol I couldn't identify. I spent hours researching it, sending photos to people, using reverse image searches, but nothing came up. The chest also had a strange history: apparently, everyone who had owned it before reported a string of bad luck. Naturally,

I dismissed that part as superstition, but it intrigued me nonetheless.

Within two weeks of owning the chest, my life was turned upside down. I narrowly avoided a horrendous car accident. It was one of those moments where, in the blink of an eye, everything could have changed. And that was just the start. My personal life unravelled rapidly. A five-year relationship, which had been solid, ended abruptly. On top of that, my events company, which had been steadily growing, started to struggle. The bookings dropped, and there was drama on social media, with people gossiping and attacking me for things beyond my control.

It was like a perfect storm of negativity, and I couldn't shake the feeling that it all traced back to the chest. Looking back now, I know it was likely just coincidence, life has its ups and downs, but at the time, it was hard not to connect the dots. Despite the overwhelming sense of bad luck, I didn't consider getting rid of the chest. If anything, it pushed me deeper into investigating it. I wanted to understand whether there was something more to its story, something paranormal, or just a strange sequence of events tied to this old, mysterious object.

By the summer of 2018, I was in a really bad place. The Haunted Hunts events had come to a halt after I'd stopped running them entirely. My career, which had felt like it was on the verge of something bigger, had stalled completely, and I had no idea how to get it back on track.

Instead of focusing on what to do next, I found myself spiralling. I spent most nights out drinking, going on massive benders that left me feeling worse each morning. It wasn't just the financial cost, although I wasted a lot of money, it was the emotional toll. I felt completely lost, like I had no direction, no purpose. For the first time, I fully stepped away from the paranormal world. I didn't even recognise myself anymore.

Then I met Alice. I don't want to say she "saved" me, but she certainly brought a calmness into my life that I hadn't felt in a long time. Alice wasn't really into the paranormal when we first met, in fact, she knew very little about it. But her curiosity was infectious. She'd ask me endless questions about my experiences, the investigations, and the strange things I'd seen over the years.

That genuine interest reignited something inside me, something that had been lost during my downward spiral. It was like a switch flipped. I suddenly felt like myself again. With Alice in my life, I started to piece everything back together. She gave me the stability and perspective I needed, and because of that, my ambition returned. I found myself getting back into the work I loved, back into the paranormal world, and once again chasing after the passion that had driven me for so long. Looking back, I don't think I would have pulled myself out of that hole without her influence and support.

With Alice's support, I launched a new project showcasing the haunted items I'd collected, including Grace, at Tatton Old Hall, a 15th-century building located within the grounds of Tatton Park in Knutsford, Cheshire. My goal was to create an immersive space where people could not only learn about the history of the location but also dive into its paranormal side. I wanted them to experience the kind of investigations I was doing, involving research involving the collection of haunted items. It was a chance to share the unsettling experiences I'd had with Grace months earlier and see if others would encounter the same phenomena.

The Old Hall was the ideal location for this project. The building has a long-standing reputation for paranormal activity, dating back centuries, and I had already filmed an episode of 'Search for the Truth' there. It is known for its paranormal activity, with visitors and staff often reporting strange phenomena. In the original 1490 part of the house, many have experienced a strangling sensation, as if a rope was tightening around their neck, while others have heard guttural moans, loud knocking, and unexplained footsteps. Poltergeist activity is frequently reported, particularly in the Victorian dining room, and the hall is believed to be haunted by several female spirits and a powerful male entity named Tom, a violent poacher who drank himself into an early grave.

Securing the deal with Tatton Park and Cheshire East Council to gain exclusivity for running this project was a massive turning point in my career. It felt like everything had come full circle. The project at Tatton Old Hall ran successfully for years, all the way up to 2022, and during that time, it brought me a lot of attention within the paranormal community and beyond. It gave me the platform I needed to push my investigations to the next level and allowed me to share my journey with an even larger audience.

Locked down and Captured

With The Haunted Hunts new HQ firmly established at Tatton Old Hall and things back on track, I was able to focus on other opportunities that came my way. It was around this time that I got involved with 'Paranormal Lockdown UK'. Out of the blue, I received a call from Rob Saffi, the producer of the show, who had heard about me and my work in the UK. They were looking for haunted locations to feature, and it wasn't long before I found myself appearing in an episode filmed at Mill Street Barracks, one of the venues I'd been investigating for years.

'Paranormal Lockdown' was a popular US-based paranormal show featuring investigators Nick Groff and Katrina Weidman. In the show, Nick and Katrina spend 72 hours locked inside some of the world's most haunted locations, giving them extended exposure to whatever paranormal entities might linger there. The first three seasons saw the duo investigate locations across America, but for the fourth season, they shifted focus to the UK, exploring some of our most notorious haunted hotspots. The UK season kicked off with an abandoned prison in Somerset, notorious for shadow figures and strange sounds.

But for the eighth episode of 'Paranormal Lockdown UK', Nick and Katrina were set to be locked down inside Mill Street Barracks in St. Helens, a place I'd investigated many times myself. The barracks, built in 1861, have a long and haunting history. The site served as home to countless soldiers during both world wars, many of whom never returned from the frontline. After World War I, it was repurposed as an isolation unit for tuberculosis patients, housing men, women, and children. During WWII, the cellar was used as a temporary mortuary for fallen citizens and soldiers during the German bombing raids over Northern England. The bodies of hundreds of people were held there for weeks, awaiting burial.

The barracks are known for their intense paranormal activity, including reports of a former caretaker's dog, Bruce, who still haunts the grounds. In the drill hall, visitors frequently hear phantom footsteps, disembodied voices, and even the sound of marching soldiers. Tables and chairs are said to move on their own, while shouts echo through the building when it's completely empty. The basement has an especially dark reputation, with many people reporting a strong negative presence, particularly in the back rooms. There's also the ghost of a woman known as Claire, who has been seen wandering the basement's shadowy corridors.

I was asked to get involved with the episode because of my experience investigating Mill Street Barracks. Filming with Nick and Katrina was a fantastic experience. We had some great conversations about the paranormal and the different approaches to investigating, but what really struck me was the scale of their production compared to what I was used to in the UK. The Americans operate on a much larger scale, with a full team of production runners, location scouts, and tech experts working behind the scenes. It was an eye-opener for me, giving me my first real glimpse into high-level production, and it made me think about how different things could be if I had access to that kind of support for my own projects.

In the USA, they have some incredible locations and massive, sprawling buildings with their own dark pasts, but the UK has the edge when it comes to history. Our ghost stories, myths, and folklore are woven into the very fabric of our culture, and as a paranormal investigator, that's a dream come true. We're talking about castles, manor houses, ancient battlefields, and churches, all with centuries of stories behind them.

From there, my career really began to take off. I had a huge appearance on 'Unexplained: Caught on Camera', which highlighted some of my work at Tatton Old Hall, including the chilling events surrounding the Grace doll. It was surreal seeing those investigations getting so much attention, but it also gave legitimacy to what we'd captured.

Then, in 2019, I got a massive break with 'Paranormal Captured', a show that focused on analysing strange phenomena caught on film. That show was a fantastic opportunity for me and something I'll always be grateful for. It struck the perfect balance between scepticism and belief, offering both sides of the paranormal debate. I was fortunate to be one of the lead investigators, and it gave me a platform to explore locations and cases that really pushed my boundaries as a paranormal investigator.

On 'Paranormal Captured', I would head out to investigate haunted locations while a panel back in the studio analysed and commented on the footage from my investigation. The panel was a diverse mix of experts, including people like Dr. Cal Cooper, who is a respected psychologist and parapsychologist, along with other experienced paranormal investigators and behavioural experts. Their role was to offer both scientific and paranormal perspectives on the events. The following week, I'd be in the studio, critiquing someone else's investigation. This format gave viewers a balanced perspective, blending scepticism with the possibility of the unexplained. In a way, it was ahead of its time, not too dissimilar from what you see today with Danny Robins' 'Uncanny' podcast, where a story is examined from multiple viewpoints, encouraging listeners to draw their own conclusions.

Over the course of the two series, I had the chance to investigate some incredible locations. In the first series, I explored a house in Middlesbrough that had been dubbed "Hell's House," where reports of aggressive poltergeist activity had left previous residents terrified. For a winter special, I went to the infamous Jamaica Inn in Cornwall, which has long been associated with smugglers and ghostly apparitions. Then in series two, I delved into even more haunted hotspots, including the notorious Ye Olde King's Head in Chester, where I'd already had some chilling experiences. I also investigated Samlesbury Hall, a historic manor in Lancashire with a long history of ghost sightings, and Graisley Old Hall, known as "the house that cries" due to reports of eerie, unexplained sobbing echoing through its rooms.

Filming for 'Paranormal Captured' was some of the best work I've ever done. There was a real sense of professionalism on set, and despite the "team sceptic" and "team believer" dynamic, there was no animosity between the team members. Even when we were critiquing each other's investigations, it was always constructive. Everyone respected each other's opinions, and it was clear that we all shared the same passion for uncovering the truth, whether that truth was paranormal or not.

The production team at Woodcut Media was fantastic to work with - they were incredibly organised and knew how to balance the sceptical and believer angles in a way that made for compelling television. They understood that the show needed to be more than just about ghost hunting. It had to reflect the intellectual debate around the paranormal, and they did that brilliantly.

After the second series, things went quiet, and there was no talk of a third. It's a shame because I think there was potential for more. But if I've learnt one thing, it's that sometimes that's just how it goes in television. Shows come and go for reasons outside your control.

The truth is, it didn't matter that 'Paranormal Captured' wouldn't be returning because that same year, we secured a series on Amazon Prime for 'The Haunted Hunts'. It felt like everything was lifting off at once.

Entering the Fourth Dimension

With the news that 'The Haunted Hunts' had been commissioned as an Amazon Prime series, we started thinking about how to put the show together. I'd learnt a lot from the production of 'Search for the Truth', so when we began discussing how to bring 'The Haunted Hunts' to life as a series, I knew it was time to invest properly in my own production team. My sister Becki's background in television was a huge advantage. With her experience and my growing knowledge of paranormal TV, we decided to take things to the next level.

Together, we formed our own production company, Fourth Dimension Productions. Initially, we started small, releasing low-budget content on YouTube to build up our skills and reputation. It wasn't glamorous, but it gave us a solid foundation. Those early projects were our training ground, where we worked out how to balance storytelling with authenticity, as well as the technical aspects of production.

Using what we'd learnt from YouTube, we created a pilot for 'The Haunted Hunts' that captured the essence of what we wanted to achieve: a raw, investigative approach to ghost hunting. We wanted it to feel real and grounded, not overly dramatised like some of the shows out there. With the help of a contact who had worked with Amazon Prime, we managed to get our foot in the door, and the rest, as they say, is history.

I rethought the team for 'The Haunted Hunts'. Becki remained an essential part of the group, not just for her investigative skills but for her expertise in research and production. Sian and Connor, who had been with us during 'Search for the Truth', had to leave due to other commitments. Sian, in particular, found it difficult to keep up with the demanding schedule because of her busy family life, and Connor's technical expertise was pulled in other directions with work. Their departure was a loss, but it gave us the chance to bring in new energy.

That's when we brought in Emma Dawe as Sian's replacement. Emma had originally been part of The Haunted Hunts events team, joining us in 2018 after a collaboration at Newsham Park. She had a background in paranormal investigating and research, and right from the start, we clicked. Emma's investigative skills stood out immediately, and she brought a lot to the team. It was clear she would be a great addition, and her experience in the field made her a perfect fit for the new series.

Over the years, several people had come and gone from The Haunted Hunts events team, as is often the case with these kinds of groups. Many joined expecting non-stop excitement, only to quickly realise how much hard work and patience goes into organising and investigating events. Once they saw the long hours behind the scenes, the setup, takedown, and detailed planning, they often realised it wasn't for them. But Emma was different - she embraced all aspects of it. As others came and went, the core team for the series started to solidify, and we began to focus on shaping our new show.

With 'The Haunted Hunts', I wanted each series to have a distinct theme, focusing on different types of hauntings to give viewers a broader understanding of paranormal phenomena. For series one, which we titled 'Behind the Shadows', the theme was dark and disturbing locations. The events I'd experienced at Nantclwyd y Dre and with the Grace doll had shifted my attention towards the more sinister side of hauntings, and I wanted to explore this side of the paranormal further.

I hesitate to use the word "demonic" because it's so often sensationalised and overused in paranormal television. Too many shows jump to that conclusion for the sake of drama. But 'Behind the Shadows' had a clear focus on locations with reputations for housing negative or oppressive entities, what some might call demonic or malevolent. Rather than feeding into the typical narrative, I wanted to take a rational approach and investigate what was really behind these darker hauntings. Were they truly evil, or was there something else at play? perhaps misunderstood energies or misinterpreted phenomena? That was the driving force behind the first series.

One of the standout locations was Pool Park Asylum in North Wales, which had this eerie, oppressive atmosphere the moment we arrived. The building had a brutal history, first as a mental asylum and later as a World War II POW camp. What made it even more disturbing were the reports of satanic rituals taking place there, which supposedly triggered demonic activity. Our investigation was focused on finding out what, if anything, still lurked there. It was the first episode of the series, and it set the tone for everything that followed.

Then there was the Ancient Ram Inn, one of the most famously haunted locations in the country and a place I'd wanted to investigate for years. Allegedly built on a pagan burial ground, it's reputedly haunted by everything from a witch to children whose skeletal remains were found buried on the property. There's also talk of two demonic entities residing there. The Ancient Ram Inn has this reputation for being one of the scariest places you can investigate, and after spending the night there, I have to admit, it's certainly got a special character.

We also headed to Antwerp Mansion in Manchester. It's a historic house, but what really drew us there was the disturbing reports of aggression linked to the building's basement. People who spent time down there seemed to become unusually violent, and there were multiple sightings of a dark mass lurking in the lower levels. The location had a reputation for being a bit of a magnet for negative energy, and we wanted to get to the bottom of what was really happening there. It was one of our more unpredictable investigations because we didn't know how the energy in that building would affect us.

Delamere Forest was another tough one for us. We spent an entire night deep in the woods, which are believed to be haunted by spirits tied to satanic rituals. For years, people have been performing these rituals out there, and the locals are convinced the forest is cursed. Investigating a place like that, where there are no walls or doors and the paranormal activity could come from any direction, was a real test for the team. The forest had this overwhelming silence at times that almost felt more intense than the activity itself.

Then we investigated an old cotton mill with a dark history. There had been murders, suicides, and satanic rituals performed there, particularly during the 1980s. Recently, it had become known for its hauntings, but nothing prepared us for what we encountered during our lockdown there. The energy in that building was heavy, and I'd say it was one of the most intense investigations we've ever done.

Finally, we tackled what we called "Masons' Manor." At the time, we couldn't name the location due to restrictions, but most people now know it was Woolton Hall in Liverpool. The building had been used for secret Masonic meetings, and there had been recent reports of paranormal activity ramping up inside. There had been break-ins, and again, rumours of satanic rituals. This was our final lockdown of the series, and it was one of the most challenging.

After the success of series one, we were commissioned for a second series, which launched on Amazon Prime in March 2019 and took us in a new direction. Titled 'Civitas Spirituum', the series took us to Chester, a city I'd come to label "the city of spirits."

We'd seen a huge response to series one, and I knew we had to push the envelope for this next one, so we decided to focus entirely on one place. Chester, with its history as one of the oldest cities in Britain, was the perfect setting. It was originally a Roman settlement and later became one of the busiest sea ports in the country. It's a city packed with haunted locations. Everywhere you turn, there's another building with a ghost story. The idea was to spend two weeks there, investigating as much as we could and really getting under the skin of its paranormal reputation.

Unlike a typical ghost-hunting show where each episode is a standalone investigation, 'Civitas Spirituum' followed us across multiple locations throughout Chester. We didn't want to just show a collection of investigations, we wanted to take viewers on a journey through the city, blending its history with the paranormal claims tied to it.

We filmed interviews with local experts and eyewitnesses, giving context to each location we investigated. We also shot some behind-the-scenes footage of the team back at the hotel so viewers could see what happens between investigations. It was a more immersive experience, and we approached it in a way that felt like a documentary series but still kept those familiar night-vision investigations that people love.

The first episode, 'City of Spirits', was all about setting the scene. Becki and I arrived in Chester, and one of the first places we visited was St. John's Church, just outside the city walls. We met with Liz Roberts, a local historian, who gave us an incredible insight into Chester's haunted history.

The first lockdown of the series took us back to a familiar location, Ye Olde King's Head. We'd investigated this 17th-century inn before, but it was our first time back since 2017. The history of the building is fascinating, especially the discovery of a 17th-century sword during a refurbishment in 1924. There's speculation that this sword could be the reason behind the hauntings, and we were keen to explore that theory. The atmosphere in Ye Olde King's Head is always intense, and we had some interesting activity during that investigation.

Next up was The Pied Bull, Chester's oldest coaching inn. This place had a completely different energy. There are stories of a tragic accident in the cellar many years ago, and we focused a lot of our investigation on that area. As always, the cellar was dark, claustrophobic, and unnerving, but we wanted to see if we could make contact with whatever or whoever might still linger there.

From there, we headed to The George & Dragon, which threw a surprise at us. The pub is said to be built on a Roman cemetery, and there are stories of an army of Roman soldiers haunting the place. There's a lot of folklore surrounding Roman ghosts, and we wanted to dig into whether there was any truth behind those sightings. Roman history is woven into the fabric of Chester, so it wouldn't have been surprising to find traces of that energy still lingering in the city.

One of the most memorable investigations of series two took us to Rowton Moor, just outside Chester. This was the site of one of the bloodiest battles of the English Civil War, and it's said to be haunted by the ghosts of soldiers who died there. Becki and I went to

Rowton to investigate claims of ghostly sightings on the moor, and it was an intense experience.

The final episode took us to the Dewa Roman Experience, a museum in the heart of Chester built on top of Roman ruins. This investigation felt like the culmination of everything we'd been exploring throughout the series, Chester's deep connection to its Roman past and the paranormal energy that seems to flow through the city. We set out on the series asking one big question: is Chester truly the city of spirits? By the end, I think we'd found some compelling evidence to suggest it just might be.

Shadow Of The Hill

Series three marked a turning point for 'The Haunted Hunts'. This was the moment when everything shifted, and it was largely due to the decision to focus on one of the most infamous locations in English history, Pendle Hill. Pendle Hill had always fascinated me. Long before I became a paranormal investigator, its dark history and association with the witch trials called me.

Known for its dark association with the Pendle witches, the hill has long been a place shrouded in mystery and fear. The six-episode series premiered on Amazon Prime in October 2020 and quickly became our biggest success to date. Within weeks, it had racked up over three million views, making it the most popular series we had ever produced. It was a game-changer, both for the show and for me personally, as we delved into one of the darkest chapters of English history.

We wanted to take everything we'd learnt from the previous two series and apply it to one of the most notoriously haunted locations in the UK. The history surrounding Pendle Hill is chilling. Back in 1612, during the reign of King James I, England was gripped by a fear of witchcraft and the supernatural. Witch trials were common, and those accused were often executed in brutal fashion.

Twelve locals were accused of witchcraft, and ten of them were hanged. These people weren't evil, they were victims of the fear and superstition of the time, they became scapegoats in a time of paranoia and fear. To this day, many believe that the area around Pendle Hill is still haunted by the spirits of those who were executed. And that's what makes Pendle Hill so haunting. You're not just investigating ghosts, you're investigating the suffering and fear that still lingers there after all these centuries.

For me and the team, this wasn't just another investigation. This was something bigger. Pendle Hill is often regarded as one of the most haunted places in Britain, and it was a location that carried a lot of emotional weight for us. The story of those accused of witchcraft has haunted generations, and we were determined to explore whether their spirits still linger in the area.

One of the reasons we were so excited about releasing this series was because we knew we had captured something extraordinary on camera. During the investigation, we believe we caught a full-bodied apparition on film, something that is incredibly rare in paranormal investigations. It's by far the best piece of evidence we've ever captured, and it was a moment that left the entire team in shock. We couldn't believe what we were seeing, and we couldn't wait to share it with the audience. This wasn't just a fleeting shadow or a light anomaly. This was something far more substantial, and it really validated everything we were doing.

Each episode took us deeper into the history and the hauntings. We explored the locations surrounding Pendle Hill, including the places where the accused witches were said to live and meet. These were locations steeped in dark history, and standing in those very spots brought the human tragedy of the witch trials to life in a haunting way. We weren't just trying to document paranormal activity, we were trying to connect with the past to understand the fear and hysteria that led to the brutal executions. Through this approach, we felt a deeper connection to the locations, and in doing so, we found what we believe to be some of the most compelling evidence of the paranormal that we've ever captured.

One of the major innovations we introduced in the third series was a device I designed myself, called the IntraVox. Its creation stemmed from my growing frustration with the so-called "ghost hunting" gadgets that have become standard in paranormal investigations. Every time I saw people turning up to events with K-II meters, REM-Pods, spirit boxes, and other gadgets, it reinforced my belief that there needed to be more education around what works in an investigation and what doesn't.

These devices, while popular, don't offer anything close to definitive proof of paranormal activity. The K-II meter, for example, is designed to detect electromagnetic fields (EMFs), but the problem is it can also pick up on everyday electronics, leading to countless false positives.

I can say this with confidence because I've used all of these devices myself. Over the years, I've tried and tested everything out there - Ovilus, Alice Boxes, SLS cameras, K-II meters, you name it. Through countless investigations, I've gathered a wealth of experience using this equipment, and what I've seen consistently is how little it contributes to the validity of a paranormal investigation.

For me, this reliance on flashy tech often leads to more confusion than clarity. I wanted to create something that moved away from that. The IntraVox was born out of that desire to strip things back, focus on simplicity, and create something that could truly help further the investigation, rather than just adding more noise. The goal was to eliminate the outside interference that comes with devices like spirit boxes and focus on a more controlled method of potentially capturing paranormal communication.

Take the Ovilus, for example, a device that claims to translate environmental energy into words. What it actually offers is a random series of words with no real connection to what's happening in the environment. The Alice Box works on a similar principle, but again, the results are far from definitive. The SLS camera, which uses infrared sensors to map out human shapes, often mistakes objects like door frames or furniture for figures, resulting in highly questionable "evidence." But despite my scepticism, I'm a firm believer in not dismissing something without testing it first. I've given all these gadgets a fair shot, and each time, the results have only confirmed what I suspected from the start: these devices are not providing the reliable evidence people think they are.

One device I tried extensively was a spirit box, a device that scans rapidly through AM and FM radio frequencies, creating bursts of static interspersed with fragments of radio broadcasts. The theory behind their use is that spirits can somehow manipulate the random radio signals to form words or even complete sentences, relaying messages from the other side. Many ghost hunters who use spirit boxes believe that the garbled noises or disjointed words they hear are direct communication from the dead. But I've always been sceptical of this interpretation. In my view, what's really happening is a case of audio pareidolia. This is a psychological phenomenon where our brains are wired to find patterns in random sounds or images. When faced with random noise, our minds try to make sense of it by hearing familiar words or phrases, often shaped by our own expectations. So, when someone believes a spirit is trying to communicate, they're more likely to hear what they want to hear, even though there's no real evidence to support the idea that spirits can manipulate radio waves in this way.

Still, I wanted to explore the potential of white noise and its role in triggering paranormal events. Although I wasn't a big believer in spirit boxes, I started experimenting with a device called the Portal, which I got from Infraready, a respected ghost-hunting equipment shop run by Andy Bailey here in the UK. The Portal is typically used alongside spirit boxes, designed to amplify and refine the output, reducing the distracting bursts of radio chatter. What really caught my attention, though, was how it filtered out most of the radio broadcast, leaving behind the white noise, the static between stations that many believe might serve as a conduit for spirit communication.

White noise has long been linked to the idea that spirits can manipulate energy to make their presence known, and this intrigued me. I wasn't expecting much, but almost immediately after turning it on, something started happening. In different locations, we would hear unexplained sounds like footsteps in empty rooms, knocks, and even faint voices. It was enough to get me thinking more seriously about the potential role white noise might play in paranormal phenomena.

I remember testing the Portal at Tatton Old Hall, and within minutes of turning it on, we began hearing unexplained noises throughout the building like footsteps in the halls, knocks coming from empty rooms, and occasional loud bangs. The activity seemed to increase in intensity, almost as if the white noise was agitating or triggering something in the environment. It felt as though the static was stirring up the energy in the space, encouraging the activity to manifest.

This was the moment that sparked the idea for the IntraVox. I started thinking: what if the spirit box wasn't the key to unlocking communication, but the white noise itself? Could it be that the static, rather than any manipulation of radio frequencies, was actually creating the right conditions for paranormal events to unfold? It seemed plausible, and I became determined to explore this theory further, focusing on how white noise might act as a catalyst for activity rather than just relying on devices like the spirit box.

I decided to take matters into my own hands and began developing a device that could harness the potential of white noise without depending on the flawed and easily manipulated spirit box. The process wasn't quick, it took me several months of trial and error, with two failed prototypes, before I finally cracked it on the third attempt. That's when the IntraVox was born. Unlike a spirit box, which scans through AM and FM radio frequencies and can pick up stray broadcasts, the IntraVox operates on a completely different principle. I created a custom bank of frequencies and white noise sound banks using software called Reason, which allowed me to control every aspect of the audio. This meant that there was no external interference, no chance of picking up stray radio stations or any internet signals. Everything coming out of the IntraVox was pure, generated sound, leaving no room for outside contamination. It was as close to a controlled environment as I could get.

I began field-testing the IntraVox, and the results were nothing short of remarkable. Almost immediately, the phenomena I'd experienced with the Portal resurfaced. We'd hear unexplained footsteps echoing in empty buildings, loud banging sounds emanating from areas where no one was present, and, most intriguingly, voices that seemed to exist within the very atmosphere of the room. These weren't disembodied voices picked up by a spirit box or through an EVP (electronic voice phenomena) recorder, they were clear, audible voices heard in real-time by everyone present.

The fact that these experiences were documented on camera with multiple eyewitnesses only strengthened my belief that I was on to something with the IntraVox. I started to think that the device wasn't just triggering paranormal phenomena, it was possibly influencing the environment or the structure of the building itself, creating vibrations or disturbances that led to these events. It felt like we were tapping into something deeper, something that could provide a tangible connection to the paranormal.

To this day, the IntraVox remains one of the most valuable tools in my arsenal. Some of the most compelling evidence I've ever captured throughout my entire career has come while using this device. I'm not claiming it's definitive proof of the paranormal, but the results it produces open up new avenues for exploration in our quest for answers. Unlike many of the gadgets on the market that are prone to generating false positives or misleading data, the IntraVox is grounded in rational experimentation and careful observation. That's what sets it apart and makes it an essential part of my investigations.

Toxic Undercurrents

2020 was a challenging year for everyone due to the pandemic, but it brought an unexpected silver lining for us in the paranormal field. With people stuck at home, streaming content became a lifeline, and I saw a massive surge in interest around paranormal investigations. Viewers were looking for an escape, something intriguing to watch, and paranormal content filled that void.

I wasn't the only one who noticed this surge, others in the field reported the same. It wasn't just casual curiosity anymore, people were diving deeper into the genre, watching multiple shows, and becoming more invested in paranormal investigations. This surge in viewership translated into a growing audience for 'The Haunted Hunts'.

For me personally, the pandemic was a bit of a blessing in disguise. Although it was an incredibly difficult time for the world, it allowed people to discover my work, follow my shows, and become part of the journey. Looking back, it was a pivotal time for my career, and it set the stage for everything that came next.

But while most of the country was 'clapping for carers' and trying to spread positivity and love during lockdown, something darker was bubbling beneath the surface in the paranormal world. Although everything seemed to be going well for me on the surface, there was a shift happening that I hadn't fully experienced before.

Over the course of a few months, I started noticing a growing undercurrent of drama within the paranormal community, an unsettling amount of it. Now, I'd seen small spats between event companies before, but once my profile began to grow and my work reached a larger audience, the negativity and animosity directed toward me became relentless. People I didn't even know were attacking my credibility, questioning my work, and, in some cases, spreading outright lies. It was eye-opening and disheartening to see how quickly people could turn on you in a field where you'd expect a sense of camaraderie.

It reminded me of the psychomagnotheric slime flowing beneath New York in 'Ghostbusters II'. In the film, the slime grows stronger by feeding off the hostility and negative emotions of the city's residents. It felt like the paranormal community had its own version of that slime, thriving on drama and conflict. The more I put myself out there, the more it seemed to grow, and before I knew it, I was at the centre of it all. Just like in the film, it was as if the negativity was spreading, fuelled by people's egos, rivalries, and grudges, and it became nearly impossible to escape from.

It all started with anonymous messages popping up in my inbox, and soon after, fake Facebook profiles began leaving nasty comments about me on social media. At first, I brushed it off, thinking it was just the occasional online troll, something most people in the public eye deal with. But it quickly became clear that this was more than just a few isolated incidents. Other well-known investigators were facing similar attacks. Groups and shows that were gaining traction became targets, and it seemed like the better they did, the more vicious the backlash. I began to realise that a significant portion of the paranormal community wasn't just vocal, they were actively negative. It wasn't the friendly rivalry you'd expect, but something far more toxic. The only explanation that made sense was jealousy. People were watching others succeed in ways they hadn't or couldn't, and it was breeding resentment. That bitterness manifested in constant attacks, creating a community that thrived on tearing others down rather than supporting each other.

This wasn't just the occasional negative comment. It was a relentless wave of trolling. New fake profiles would appear almost daily, and these people seemed disturbingly obsessed. No matter what I posted or where I showed up, they were there, ready to criticise and tear me down. It wasn't enough for them to just watch from the sidelines, they were actively looking for ways to attack me.

It became exhausting, especially when they'd swarm on any positive comment someone made about me. If a fan shared something supportive in a group, these trolls would immediately pile on, like a pack of vultures. It felt like a gang mentality, and I couldn't wrap my head around why it was happening. What made it even worse was how personal it became, they weren't just attacking my work, they were coming after me as a person. The constant barrage started to chip away at my mental health, and for a while, it really got to me.

I had never experienced anything like it before. What made it even harder to process was that many of these trolls were prominent figures in the paranormal community, acting like children despite being fully grown adults in their 40s or 50s. It was baffling. These were people I had respected from a distance, and now I was seeing a side of them that felt shockingly immature and petty.

In my mind, a lot of them must have been carrying unresolved issues from their past, possibly from being bullied, and were now projecting that pain in their adult life. I know that might not be the most politically correct way of putting it, but it's something I stand by. There's definitely an element of mental health struggles within the paranormal field, and this toxic behaviour only reinforced that belief for me. It was like a perfect storm of insecurity and bitterness, and I began to see that this wasn't just a one-off issue, there was something deeply unhealthy bubbling beneath the surface of this community.

I was around 30 at the time, and I had never encountered anything like this in my life. It was shocking to see adults, people much older than me, acting like schoolchildren, going so far as to create fake profiles just to hurl abuse. Maybe it was because I was younger and gaining recognition quickly, but I couldn't understand why people were so bothered by me.

Some of the comments were incredibly personal and had nothing to do with my actual work. I'd see things like, "I don't like this chav," "Who does he think he is?" or "I've been in this field for 30 years, and this jumped-up little shit comes along." Others solely targeted my investigation style, which baffled me because, in the paranormal world, there's no rulebook. Every investigator brings their own methods, and that's how the field evolves. Yet here I was, being torn down for doing things differently.

Some of the criticism centred around the idea that I was "confrontational to spirits," which, from a sceptical standpoint, is laughable. How can you be confrontational with something that hasn't even been scientifically proven to exist? Yet these critics were adamant that I was being disrespectful to the dead, which, to me, didn't make sense at all. I'm not there to hold a séance or make friends with ghosts. I'm there to provoke a response and see if something happens. In my mind, a more provocative approach was just another method of testing the boundaries of paranormal phenomena.

In the early days of my investigations, I wasn't afraid to challenge whatever might be there, pushing for an interaction. Most people who attended our events or watched the show supported this approach, recognising it as a legitimate way of seeking evidence. I adopted this approach because I was tired of seeing the same dull, ineffective techniques used in investigations.

Over and over, investigators would call out to spirits in the same monotonous way, asking, "Are there any spirits here with us?" But that question always struck me as flawed: how would a spirit even know it's a spirit? It was as if people were just copying what they'd seen on shows like 'Most Haunted', where investigators would ask the same passive, repetitive questions without much thought.

I wanted to shake things up and introduce something different. If we're dealing with intelligent entities, there's a good chance they might not even know they're dead. So I approached investigations as if I were interacting with a living person, bringing a more provocative energy and challenging them. My hope was that this different approach might trigger a response or push the boundaries in ways that conventional methods never seemed to.

And it worked. The feedback from people attending my events or watching my shows was overwhelmingly positive. I'd often hear things like, "Keep doing it. It's working!" People appreciated the fresh energy I brought to investigations, and for the most part, they found it exciting and engaging.

Despite this, that small percentage of negativity - maybe just 5% - was the loudest and most persistent. While 95% of the feedback was positive, it was the critical voices that really got under my skin. And it wasn't just people disagreeing with my methods. It became personal as the attacks went beyond my investigation style, questioning my character, my motives, and even my right to be in the field. I couldn't understand it. I wasn't breaking any rules, there are no rules in this field. So why were people reacting with such hostility?

I didn't let it change me, though. I stuck to my guns and continued using the approach I believed in. But the trolling became so obsessive and relentless that I had to do something about it. At that stage of my life, I had never experienced anything like this before, and I had no PR training or any experience in handling public backlash.

I come from a background where, if you've got an issue with someone, you deal with it face to face. So encountering this kind of behaviour with people hiding behind screens and sending abuse anonymously was completely foreign to me. So, I reacted the only way I knew how, like I would in a real-life confrontation.

My instinct was to stand my ground. I thought, "No, I'm not going to stand for this. If you've got something to say, come and say it to my face." I openly called them out, told them to stop hiding behind their keyboards, and challenged them to have a real conversation. Looking back, I can see now that it was the wrong approach. In the world of social media, where people thrive on anonymity and drama, engaging with trolls only feeds their fire.

By responding, I only made things worse. It was like throwing fuel on the fire, and my reactions seemed to trigger even more people to get involved. Suddenly, online drama spats became a regular occurrence, with new trolls popping up and feeding off each interaction. It started to take a toll on my mental health, and I found myself consumed by it, constantly checking social media, dreading what I'd see next. Eventually, I had to learn the hard way that the only way to handle these people was to block them and move on. Engaging with them gave them exactly what they wanted: attention. I realised that what was really bothering them wasn't anything I was actually doing, it was the fact that my work was getting noticed. That's what wound them up, and the jealousy and resentment just snowballed from there.

The drama in the paranormal community is something I hear about constantly. Whether I'm at conventions, public investigations, or just chatting with people, they'll often say, "I don't know how you deal with this." Many others have faced the same kind of issues, and it seems that anyone involved in events, online content, or any form of public paranormal work will encounter this negativity at some point.

It's not limited to just me, it's a community-wide problem. What's really strange is that it's often the people who claim to be passionate about the paranormal who are the most toxic. They attack those who succeed, and instead of supporting each other or growing the field, they turn it into a battleground of egos. It's almost as if the more public you are, the more you become a target for this kind of behaviour.

Now, I know how to handle it. I keep my head down and focus on the work, refusing to let the trolls distract me from what drew me to the paranormal in the first place. Alongside the negativity, there have been countless positives that remind me why I'm passionate about this field. 'The Haunted Hunts' series on Amazon Prime was a huge success, reaching audiences far beyond what I ever imagined. Because of this, I started receiving invitations to paranormal conventions, radio shows, podcasts, and more. There were so many people in the industry who genuinely respected what I had accomplished and supported my work. The guys at Haunted Magazine were fantastic, as were many others in the field who, like me, weren't interested in drama. I've built solid friendships and met colleagues who truly appreciate and respect what I do. On top of that, I've had the privilege to visit and investigate some incredible locations steeped in history and the unknown, and that's a huge part of why I continue to do this.

The drama never slowed us down. When we returned a year later with series four of 'The Haunted Hunts', we were ready to take things even further. The series was called 'Project Invocation', and was unlike anything we'd ever done before. The series pushed the entire team to their limits, both mentally and emotionally.

The concept behind 'Project Invocation' was simple but terrifying: could human fear itself be the catalyst for paranormal activity? There's a belief that fear can conjure a supernatural entity, or at the very least, drive any existing entities to become more active. But we also knew that fear has a way of messing with your mind, making you see and hear things that might not really be there. That fine line between genuine paranormal activity and the tricks fear plays on your brain was what we set out to explore.

Going into the series, I knew this was going to be a whole new challenge for the team. In the past, we'd had success because of our research and tactical approach to investigating haunted locations. But this time around, we were completely blind. We didn't know where we were going or what we'd be dealing with until the day of each investigation. The only clue we'd get was a postcode handed to us on the morning of the investigation. That made it difficult to know which techniques to use, and it kept us on edge the entire time. The lack of preparation created an atmosphere of genuine fear, and that's exactly what we wanted for 'Project Invocation'.

The team were pushed outside of their comfort zones with terrifying lone vigils, sensory deprivation experiments, and situations that were specifically designed to play on our fears. It was intense, and at times, it was overwhelming. I think I can comfortably say that all of us had moments in this series that genuinely scared us. In fact, it brought one of the team members to tears at one point. 'Project Invocation' didn't just test our ability to investigate the paranormal. It tested how far we could push ourselves psychologically.

One of the most fascinating aspects of this series was seeing how the power of imagination can take over when you're in a horrible situation. When you're plunged into darkness and isolated in a location you know nothing about, your mind starts filling in the blanks. We had some incredible moments of debunking things that initially seemed paranormal but turned out to be tricks of the mind. At the same time, there were moments when it felt like our fear was actually stirring something up, like the energy we were putting out was being answered by the locations we were investigating.

What made 'Project Invocation' even more unique was the way it was structured. Back at HQ, my partner Alice and Nick Anderson were responsible for setting our assignments and tasks. Fans had seen glimpses of them in series three, but this time they really became part of 'The Haunted Hunts' family. They absolutely tortured us throughout the filming process, sending us into some incredibly unsettling situations, but they were a huge credit to the success of the series. Having them behind the scenes while we were out in the field gave the show a different dynamic, and it really added to the tension, knowing they were the ones deciding how far we'd be pushed.

I think what made 'Project Invocation' stand out was that it wasn't just about the paranormal. It was about fear, the mind, and how those two things can intertwine. We'd had great success with series three, and I knew fans had high expectations, so I was excited to see how they'd react to this completely new format. Even though it was different, I think it delivered just as much as the previous series. It was terrifying, unpredictable, and pushed us further than we'd ever gone before.

We kept the momentum up with series five, subtitled 'Cemeteries of the Dead', which premiered on Amazon Prime in the spring of 2022. The theme for this season revolved around burial sites, and we set out to see if there was a connection between the dead and the lingering paranormal activity at these haunted locations. Each place we visited had a deep link to death and burial, whether through cemeteries, discovered skeletons, or tragic deaths. We explored everything from family homes with pet cemeteries to historical halls with grim discoveries of dismembered body parts.

One of the standout locations was Bishton Hall in Staffordshire. This place started life as a grand 18th-century family home before becoming a prep school, and it's now rapidly gaining a reputation as one of

Staffordshire's most haunted places. The reports we received before heading there included phantom footsteps, disembodied voices, doors opening and closing by themselves, and even the sound of a woman screaming. One of the most unnerving aspects of this location is the pet cemetery on the grounds, which adds a layer of creepiness. The sightings of dark mists and shadowy figures at Bishton Hall weren't just stories, some of us saw them with our own eyes.

Another deeply historical location we visited was Norton Priory in Runcorn, where the remains of 130 skeletons were found during an excavation. The priory, dating back to the 12th century, is now mostly in ruins, but its history is haunting. There are frequent reports of shadowy figures roaming the grounds, disembodied screams, and even a skull-like face that has been seen in the undercroft. Investigating a place tied so closely to death and burial made us wonder if the spirits of those 130 people might still be tied to the priory, their energy trapped in the ruins.

At Walton Hall in Warrington, we were faced with a different kind of haunting. The hall is known for its ghostly children, with many visitors reporting the sounds of children laughing, crying, and running up and down the stairs. There are also stories of Lady Daresbury, whose ghost is said to haunt her former bedroom. Visitors claim that if she doesn't like you, you'll have a particularly unpleasant experience, and some have even been pushed out of her room.

We also investigated Penrhyn Old Hall in Conwy, a place that has seen more than its fair share of death. The hall dates back to the early 15th century and is infamous for its tales of murder, dismembered bodies, and skeletons. The most famous ghosts reported here are those of a young girl murdered by her sisters for wanting to marry outside the Catholic faith and a phantom monk who roams the building. We also encountered reports of a bad-tempered spirit of a man, mischievous child ghosts, and even the spirit of a soldier.

One of the more interesting locations we visited was Mill Street Barracks in Merseyside. I was already familiar with this location, but we returned because the cellar was so closely linked with death. It had been used as a mortuary and held the bodies of citizens and soldiers who had died in air raids.

Finally, we wrapped up the series at Samlesbury Hall in Preston, a location with a history dating back to 1384. One of the most chilling legends associated with the hall is that of a priest who died there. Ever since his death, a mysterious bloodstain has been said to appear on the floor of the room where he died. Samlesbury Hall is a place where history and hauntings collide, and the energy inside the building seemed tied to the many tragic events that have taken place there over the centuries.

Burying the Dead

Things were going great for the team on the surface. The events company was thriving, we had a growing fanbase, and 'The Haunted Hunts' was becoming a well-known name in the paranormal field. It felt like everything was falling into place. But, as with any success, there were challenges lurking within the team. Behind the scenes, things weren't as smooth as they appeared.

As things progressed, I started to notice a shift. Ego was creeping in, and certain actions behind the scenes were starting to jeopardise both the events side of the business and the production of the Amazon Prime series. Some team members were creating tension and division, causing a lot of stress within the company.

It became clear that this kind of fallout was more common in the paranormal world than I'd originally thought. Over the years, speaking to other big names at conventions, I've learnt that internal conflicts and clashing egos can be a real problem in paranormal teams. It's something that happens more often than you'd expect, bringing a wave of toxicity with it.

In my case, the division wasn't directly tied to the show but rather stemmed from the events side of things. Friendships were forming between certain team members and regular guests, leading to cliques and, ultimately, backstabbing. It affected how the events company was being run. People I had brought on board for the ride were suddenly telling me how to run my own business, which was a situation I wasn't prepared to tolerate. Things escalated when I started receiving evidence in the form of messages and screenshots of conversations, proving that these individuals were badmouthing not just me but also regular guests who had been part of the Haunted Hunts community for years. It became clear that there was an agenda at play, one that aimed to divide the guests and stir up tension within the group.

Things escalated even further when I brought in two new team members to help manage the North Wales division of the events company. This decision sparked clear jealousy among some of the existing team members, and the situation became more toxic. Once again, I was shown evidence of conversations where they were plotting behind my back, trying to form their own team and effectively hijack the customer base I had built over the years.

They weren't just dissatisfied, they wanted to start their own company and take everything I had worked so hard to establish. It was a blatant attempt to undermine the foundation I'd laid for The Haunted Hunts, and it left me feeling betrayed. It was frustrating to see people I had trusted and given opportunities to, now trying to pull the rug out from under me.

Then there was another issue that really began to eat away at me: fakery. It's a problem that plagues the paranormal field, especially in TV shows where the pressure to deliver dramatic moments is high. But when it started happening within 'The Haunted Hunts' team, it became a line I wasn't willing to cross. One particular team member was trying to fabricate paranormal events, forcing "moments" that just weren't real. Every investigation seemed to feature some attempt to stage an incident that clearly wasn't paranormal. Whether it was manipulating equipment or exaggerating reactions, it was all about drawing attention to themselves, and I couldn't stand for it.

In the paranormal world, fakery often stems from the desire to gain attention. Unfortunately, some people see it as an easy way to gain fame, boost their profile, or make a name for themselves. There are numerous examples in the field of teams or individuals who stage events for the sake of making their investigations seem more exciting. But for me, integrity has always been at the heart of what I do. If you're faking things, you're not investigating, you're just creating entertainment at the expense of the truth. That's not what I'm about, and it's not what 'The Haunted Hunts' was supposed to be about either.

Eventually, the troublesome team members left, and with them went the toxic atmosphere that had been suffocating both the events and the show. It felt like a weight had been lifted, and for the first time in a while, I was able to see clearly where things needed to go next. It was a relief not only for me but for the remaining team members as well. This was the perfect moment to shake things up and bring a fresh approach to both the events company and 'The Haunted Hunts' show itself.

Around the same time, we had just signed a new contract with Amazon Prime, which gave us the perfect opportunity to reimagine the show. I wanted to take everything I'd learnt from the past series, the successes and the mistakes, and use that to create something more engaging and authentic.

The previous five series had carved out a solid foundation, and they certainly had their place in our journey, but we were ready for something more, something that would push not only ourselves but also our audience to think more critically about the paranormal. Because this new series was going to be so different from what we had done before, it made sense to reset the counter. We decided to start fresh, launching this as a brand-new series one, with a completely revamped format that would set a new tone for 'The Haunted Hunts'. It was the start of a new chapter for us, both on and off screen, and it felt like the right direction to take.

This new version of 'The Haunted Hunts' had a very different focus. Instead of sticking to famous haunted locations, which had been the bread and butter of previous series, we shifted our attention to callout cases. We wanted to help everyday people who were experiencing strange phenomena in their homes and businesses, places that don't necessarily have a well-documented paranormal history but where something was clearly happening. The goal was to put education before entertainment, emphasising investigation techniques, rational thinking, and critical analysis over the sensationalism that often dominates paranormal shows.

The new direction felt more personal and grounded, giving us the opportunity to explore what was really going on in these spaces. Rather than simply presenting ghost stories, we were aiming to provide the tools and knowledge for people to understand what they were experiencing. I wanted to push the boundaries of what a paranormal show could be by showing viewers how real investigations unfold without the overhyped drama or faked moments often found in the genre.

The team behind this new series, Becki, Emma, Alice, Nick, and myself, had already developed a strong dynamic while working together since series two of the original show. We'd been through so much together, from tough investigations to the behind-the-scenes challenges, and I knew this was the group I wanted to take on this new journey. Each person brought something unique to the table, and our combined skills meant we were able to offer a balanced, critical approach to every case we took on.

I was excited to share this new direction with our fans, knowing that while it was a shift from what they were used to, it was also an opportunity to show a more thoughtful and methodical approach to paranormal investigation that often gets overlooked, as we tried to make sense of what people were experiencing in their homes and businesses. I knew that this format might not appeal to those looking for pure entertainment, but I was confident it would resonate with viewers who valued a more balanced investigative approach to the paranormal. And I have to say, the response from our fans during this transition was nothing short of incredible. They stood by us, embracing the change, and stuck with us. That backing meant everything, especially during a time when we were taking a bit of a risk by moving away from the traditional haunted locations.

There were five episodes in this new series, each one offering a different kind of challenge and mystery. The first episode took us to Castle Cottage near Salisbury, Wiltshire, a location with its own eerie reputation. From there, we moved on to Sinai Park House, a historic moated house in Burton-on-Trent, Staffordshire. Sinai Park House, with its deep historical roots stretching back to the 14th century, had long been associated with paranormal activity. Over the years, it had gained a reputation as one of Staffordshire's most haunted places, with tales of ghostly monks, shadow figures, and unsettling energies tied to the building's past as a rest house for monks from nearby Burton Abbey.

As the series progressed, it became clear that viewers understood and appreciated what we were trying to achieve with this shift toward rational investigation and education. They saw that we were moving away from the more dramatic style of previous series and really honing in on the truth behind these hauntings. It wasn't about creating spectacle, it was about uncovering real stories and, if possible, providing answers to the mysteries we were investigating.

We didn't let any of the challenges that had once threatened to derail everything slow us down, including the behind-the-scenes drama. The new series was a testament to that resilience, and the overwhelmingly positive response from viewers confirmed we were heading in the right direction.

My Haunted Hotel

Around the time we were working on the new series of 'The Haunted Hunts', I was presented with a unique opportunity by Harry Achilleos, who had purchased Ye Olde King's Head back in 2011. Harry's an incredible guy - someone who shares a deep passion for the paranormal and genuinely believes in what we do. He didn't just buy the pub because it's a historic building in Chester, he bought it because of its long-standing reputation for ghostly activity. Harry is the kind of person who's all about preserving history and embracing the stories behind it, especially when it comes to the unexplained. His enthusiasm for the paranormal made him the perfect person to collaborate with, and I was immediately interested in hearing what he had in mind.

Ye Olde King's Head is a historic inn in Chester, built in 1622 and has long been known for its hauntings. It became an inn in 1717, and ever since, it has accumulated countless reports of paranormal occurrences. It's one of those places where the history feels alive, where every corner holds a ghost story, and the past seems to breathe through the walls.

Guests and staff have reported all manner of strange activity over the years. The sound of children laughing in the dead of night, the sudden movement of objects, doors slamming shut on their own, and disembodied voices have all been witnessed. Apparitions are regularly spotted wandering the corridors, and many paranormal investigators have had encounters with the notorious dark, shadowy figure said to haunt the building.

Harry's original plan for the building was ambitious. He wanted to fill Ye Olde King's Head with cameras to monitor and capture the paranormal activity 24/7. However, the logistics of running a fully functioning pub downstairs meant that his paranormal vision had to be put on hold. Managing a busy establishment while also trying to cater to paranormal investigations proved to be a difficult balancing act, so the idea was sidelined for years. It wasn't until after the pandemic, when the pub faced fewer restrictions and operations slowed down, that Harry was finally able to shift his focus entirely to the paranormal side of things and bring his dream to life.

To make this vision a reality, he brought in Brett Jones to help spearhead the project. Brett had an impressive background in designing scare attractions, which gave him a unique understanding of how to create immersive environments that would heighten guests' experiences. More importantly, Brett had extensive experience in paranormal investigations and was well-versed in the world of mediumship. His ability to identify and debunk fraudulent practices in the paranormal field was invaluable, ensuring that everything done at Ye Olde King's Head would be grounded in authentic research and investigation. With Brett on board, the project was finally set to move forward in a big way.

At that point, I was starting to feel the strain of running paranormal events. After years of dedicating myself to both events and the production of my shows, it became clear that I needed a shift in direction. I had recently hosted one of my final The Haunted Hunts events at Ye Olde King's Head, back when it was still operating solely as a hotel and pub. It was a typical investigation night for me, but little did I know it would mark a significant turning point. That evening, Harry and Brett were present, watching how I ran the event. Brett turned to Harry and said, "We need to get Danny on board for this."

I had a long history with Ye Olde King's Head, having investigated the location since 2015. Over the years, I'd developed a deep connection to the building, both because of its history and the countless paranormal encounters I'd witnessed there. Harry and I had always hit it off, we shared a mutual passion for the paranormal, and I'd even featured him in episodes of 'The Haunted Hunts' and 'Paranormal Captured'.

Harry had been trying to involve me in the project for years, which had now come to be known as My Haunted Hotel. His idea had intrigued me for a while, but back then, my schedule was too full to commit. However, this time, everything seemed to fall into place. The timing was right, and the opportunity was too good to pass up. It was the perfect chance to step away from the relentless pace of running events and focus on something new that could become a major part of the next chapter of my career.

The concept of My Haunted Hotel was simple yet groundbreaking. The idea was to give guests the opportunity to spend the night in one of the UK's most famously haunted inns, while every moment of their stay was captured on camera. But this wasn't your typical paranormal event. Instead of being guided around by a team of investigators, guests were left to their own devices, free to conduct their own investigations. What set My Haunted Hotel apart from other ghost-hunting experiences was its long-term approach, this was to be an ongoing investigation, with a 24/7 camera system monitoring every room in the building. Each guest became part of the investigation, contributing to a continuous stream of data and potential evidence rather than just participating in a one-off event.

Harry and Brett were already deep into the planning stages when I came on board, working on how the events would run and making structural changes to the building itself. There's a long-standing theory in the paranormal world that renovating or altering a building can stir up paranormal activity. We all believed in this idea, so Brett and Harry began reimagining certain rooms to see if it would trigger phenomena. The goal wasn't to make it feel like a theme park, but rather to connect with the building's past and tap into its haunted history. Brett, for instance, redesigned room five to resemble the nursery it was rumoured to have once been. The renovation took months, with late nights spent testing the format to establish whether it would work to have guests come in, stay overnight, and conduct their own investigations while cameras captured everything. It was a massive undertaking, but we were all excited to see if it could really work.

Harry's initial vision was to stream the cameras live 24/7, capturing every moment of potential paranormal activity as it unfolded. However, after joining the project, I realised this idea wasn't practical. The sheer amount of footage would have been overwhelming, not to mention the technical challenges. So, I proposed a different approach: why not turn it into a weekly show instead?

With my background in production, I knew we could create something more structured. The idea was to film the guests' investigations throughout the week and then compile the most compelling moments into weekly episodes. We had at our disposal 16 static cameras that had previously been installed throughout the building during the Covid-19 pandemic, ensuring that no corner would be left unchecked. This way, no potential paranormal event would go unnoticed. The guests became the stars of their own investigation, and the format allowed us to show the best evidence each week in a polished, well-edited highlight show.

What set My Haunted Hotel apart from traditional paranormal events was the autonomy it gave to the guests. Instead of being guided by a team of investigators, they were free to explore and conduct their own investigations on their own terms. They checked into their rooms and had full access to the building to explore its haunted history.

Meanwhile, we monitored everything from a control room, watching the camera feeds in real-time. This wasn't just a gimmick, our setup allowed us to provide immediate feedback. If a guest reported hearing a noise or seeing something unusual, we could respond instantly via walkie-talkie to either confirm or debunk what they were experiencing. For instance, if they heard creaking, we could let them know it was just the building's old pipes, or if they claimed to hear footsteps, we could check the cameras to see if it was someone else in the building or something unexplainable. This level of transparency and accuracy made the experience more credible, offering guests a chance to engage in genuine investigations with real-time insights.

The show gained traction almost immediately, and I believe a big part of that success was due to the dynamic between me, Harry, and Brett. While we were co-hosts and serious about investigating the paranormal, we didn't let the show become too dark or overly intense. Instead, we brought humour into the mix, something rarely seen in this genre. Most paranormal shows stick to a grim and serious tone, but we kept things light-hearted, with plenty of banter. It was three mates taking the mick out of each other while still conducting serious investigations, and audiences really connected with that. The balance between genuine paranormal work and comedy made the show feel different from anything else out there, and it's one of the reasons it became such a hit.

'My Haunted Hotel' quickly became a Sunday night favourite, drawing in viewers who loved the fact that it was free to watch on YouTube. This accessibility was a massive draw for fans, and there really was nothing else like it in the paranormal world. The show's growth was rapid. We found ourselves booked solid for months ahead, and the attention we received was beyond anything I had experienced before.

Offers from producers started flooding in, including interest from Discovery+, and even ITV's 'This Morning' enquired about sending presenter Josie Gibson to spend a night at the hotel for a segment. It was surreal. The exposure skyrocketed the hotel and the show to new heights, and we found ourselves at the centre of attention in the paranormal community. It was unlike anything I had ever imagined when we first launched the project.

For me, My Haunted Hotel was a complete breath of fresh air. It didn't feel like work at all, it was just three mates doing what they loved, and I was the happiest I'd ever been. We were generating headlines, and people were genuinely fascinated by the concept because it was so different from anything else out there.

From an investigative standpoint, My Haunted Hotel gave me an opportunity to conduct long-term research like never before. Having 24/7 surveillance meant that we could study the environment in ways that weren't possible during typical one-night investigations. We started noticing patterns. Things would happen at certain times of the year, during specific weather conditions. For example, I noticed patterns in paranormal activity that seemed to correlate with rain.

It also allowed us to delve into the psychological aspects of guests' experiences. Many arrived with preconceived ideas about what they were going to encounter, and more often than not, we could explain away those experiences rationally. Still, there were some phenomena that simply couldn't be debunked.

The combination of continuous monitoring, guest interaction, and historical context allowed us to analyse everything in great detail, offering a depth of research I hadn't encountered before.

The evidence we captured at My Haunted Hotel was nothing short of remarkable. We witnessed objects move on camera, like a rocking chair in room six, which had been a hotbed of paranormal reports, and a chair in the old brothel section that inexplicably shifted on its own. But one of the most jaw-dropping moments was when we caught a large black shadow figure walking down the corridor in broad daylight, fully visible in colour.

What made this capture even more intriguing was that the shadow was walking down a corridor that no longer existed in the building's current layout. It followed the path of an old corridor from a time when the inn's structure was different. This wasn't just a fleeting glimpse. It was a full-bodied shadow, moving with purpose, and to capture something that so many had reported seeing over the years was an absolute highlight of my career. It was the kind of evidence that validated everything we were doing.

The knocking on room five's door became one of the most puzzling and consistent phenomena we encountered. It wasn't just a one-off occurrence, it happened three or four times a week, without fail, and we never found a logical explanation for it. We tried everything to debunk it: checking the structure of the door, the air pressure in the room, the possibility of vibrations from outside, even changes in temperature that might cause the wood to expand or contract. But the knocking persisted, defying all our attempts to explain it away. What made it even more bizarre was that it didn't follow any predictable pattern. It could happen at any time, day or night, and even when no guests were staying in the room, the knocks would continue. To this day, it remains one of the most unsettling mysteries at the hotel, and it still baffles us.

The success of My Haunted Hotel wasn't just down to the evidence we captured but also the way we presented it. We showed the entire process, including the steps we took to debunk or explain away certain phenomena. This transparency attracted a more sceptical audience, and I think that's why the show gained so much respect. It wasn't about sensationalism, it was about real, long-term investigation, which is rare in the paranormal world. But what starts as scepticism can sometimes turn into outright attacks. It became clear that not everyone was happy with the success we were achieving.

Debunking

By the time My Haunted Hotel had been running for a while, we were starting to attract a loyal group of regular guests, and the project had evolved into much more than just a paranormal investigation show. We began hosting special events like New Year's parties and Halloween gatherings, where people could experience the hotel in a different, more festive atmosphere.

One of the best things to come out of the project has been the strong sense of community that's formed around it. We've built what we call "the My Haunted family," a dedicated group of fans and guests who travel from all over the world to be part of the experience. It's been amazing to see people come from as far as Australia, New Zealand, Canada, and America, all drawn by their fascination with the hotel and the show.

We've held open days at the hotel where people can come in, explore the location, meet the team, and ask questions about the project, the building's history, and even the production process behind the show. It's become a way to bring people together around a shared passion for the paranormal, creating a welcoming and supportive community.

One night, things were going as normal. Guests were having a great time - but what we didn't know was that one of them had actually come to try and debunk us. This guy named Beardo, who runs a YouTube channel called Beardo Gets Scared, had visited the hotel with his wife. At the time, we had no idea who he was or that he had an agenda. During his stay, he really seemed to enjoy the night, and I even managed to get him on camera saying how much he liked the place.

Of course, we had no doubt Beado would find us credible. Our investigations are transparent, and we've built a reputation on not engaging in fakery. But at the same time, there were these stories circulating online that were painting us in an unfair light, suggesting we were manipulating the activity or staging events, which simply wasn't true.

These stories date back to 2013, when Harry hosted a one-off Halloween event at Ye Olde King's Head called "Psych-Hotel." It was essentially a scare attraction, where actors dressed as zombies would jump out at guests. It was a typical Halloween-themed night designed purely for entertainment. Events like this happen annually at countless locations, even those that are known for their haunted reputation, such as Newsham Park Hospital, where guests are guided through eerie locations by actors for a spooky thrill.

But for some reason, people latched onto that one event at the hotel and twisted it to suit their own agenda. They combined it with the fact that Brett had a background in designing scare attractions, and suddenly, a narrative emerged that My Haunted Hotel was nothing more than a rebranded scare attraction. This completely false idea was pushed online, claiming that we were faking paranormal activity to scare our guests. It was complete nonsense, but once the story took hold, it became another thing we had to contend with.

To prove we were legitimate, we decided to invite Beardo back, along with Mark and Tony from Paranormal Scientific Investigators (PSI), a highly scientific ghost-hunting team based in Hull. These guys are known for their rigorous approach, and we gave them full access to the hotel. They could check anything they wanted, behind doors, inside walls, everything.

There had been ridiculous rumours circulating that we'd hidden speakers in the walls to generate spooky sounds. Not only is that idea absurd, but it would also be impossible in a Grade II-listed building like Ye Olde King's Head. The strict regulations around altering a listed building mean you can't just install whatever you like, let alone secretly rig it with sound equipment. We wanted to put those rumours to bed once and for all.

We let these guys investigate however they wanted, giving them complete freedom to explore the hotel. Three things happened that night, which left them completely stunned. First, Beardo experienced a direct voice phenomenon (DVP) in room eight. DVPs are incredibly rare disembodied voices that can be heard audibly without the need for any recording equipment. The fact that he heard one was a big moment. Then, one of the PSI team members had his t-shirt pulled, an event that we managed to capture on camera. It was an unexpected and unexplained moment. Finally, they all heard the same knocking sounds that had baffled us for so long, and despite their best efforts, they couldn't debunk it.

By the end of the night, they were all on camera, openly admitting that this place was legitimate and that no fakery was involved. Their validation was a huge win for us, as it confirmed what we already knew.

Despite that, we weren't always so lucky with other debunkers. There were many who had no real interest in conducting a proper investigation. Some of them had never even been on a paranormal investigation in their life, but they were making a lot of noise online, and none of it was positive.

After about 18 months of My Haunted Hotel seeing tremendous growth and everything going well, we suddenly started getting attacked by this new wave of debunkers. They were primarily YouTube-based, and we weren't the only ones they were targeting. There's been a noticeable rise in these paranormal debunking channels over the past few years, and they seem to attract extremely toxic communities that follow them. These debunkers don't approach things with a genuine sceptical eye - they come in with an agenda to ridicule and discredit, regardless of the evidence or effort we put in. It's frustrating because we've always prided ourselves on transparency and legitimate investigation, but to them, that didn't matter.

These debunkers pushed the false narrative that Ye Olde King's Head was a scare attraction, all based on that 2013 Halloween event. They completely ignored the fact that the hotel had been running as a normal establishment right up until 2021, when Harry launched My Haunted Hotel. What these debunkers do is create a story, put it on YouTube, and their followers believe it without doing any research of their own.

It's a problem I've noticed growing on YouTube over the past two or three years: people making videos for the sole purpose of getting views, often by spinning some kind of dramatic narrative that isn't based on reality. It's all about clickbait and controversy, and it doesn't matter to them if they're dragging people's hard work and reputations through the mud. This new wave of debunkers seemed less interested in the truth and more focused on building their own popularity.

One of the worst offenders was a guy who goes by the name "The Shape," an American YouTuber. He made a video claiming that a suit of armour in the hotel was actually a paid actor, pulling strings during an event to create fake paranormal activity. We responded with a well-executed video that completely disproved his claims, showing exactly how the footage had been captured and the circumstances around it.

He had no choice but to apologise and take down his video. But by then, the damage was already done. The drama had attracted attention, and other debunkers saw the views and engagement he'd built up, so they jumped on the bandwagon. None of them could prove any fakery was happening, because there wasn't any, but that didn't stop them from continuing to push these baseless narratives just to generate views and stir up controversy.

This kind of thing drove me mad. All our hard work, our attempts to bring a scientific approach to the paranormal, was being undermined by people who had never set foot in the hotel. They were making assumptions based on nothing but speculation. And it wasn't just us, other paranormal teams and investigators were getting the same treatment. It was like a flashback to the early days of my career when I had to deal with similar hostility online.

The truth is, debunking isn't about sitting behind a screen watching videos and drawing conclusions. If you haven't been to the location and experienced it firsthand, you can't definitively say what's real and what isn't. It was frustrating because these people were quick to criticise, but they never showed up to investigate for themselves.

For me, this was frustrating, but I learnt not to let it get to me like it had in the past. We knew we were doing everything by the book, and we were always open to inviting serious investigators and debunkers in. We let them see for themselves that we weren't staging anything. But these YouTube debunkers weren't interested in the truth, they were just after views.

The real debunking happens on-site when we investigate and explain to guests that a noise is just the pipes or a shadow is from outside. That's what true investigation is about - going to the location, examining everything thoroughly, and finding logical explanations where possible. We're the ones doing real paranormal investigations, not those making assumptions from behind a screen.

There's no denying that debunkers are a much-need part of the paranormal community. Many have made a name for themselves by exposing clearly fake paranormal YouTubers and fraud in the field. This is something I support, as all balanced paranormal investigators should too.

However, some of these debunkers have become driven, not by the pursuit of truth, but by the desire to build a popular YouTube channel. This means they'll now target anyone even vaguely well known in an attempt to piggyback off their success by debunking what they do, even if they don't actually have any valid insights into whether or not the person or team they're accusing is actually engaging in fakery.

The truth is, this is just the way YouTube works these days. Controversy and drama get clicks. But I've learnt to let our work speak for itself and focus on the people who genuinely believe in what we're doing. We've built a community around My Haunted Hotel, full of people who appreciate the transparency and the effort we put into our investigations.

There will always be noise from the naysayers, but it's the real experiences we're capturing, the loyal guests who keep coming back, and the support from our community that drives us forward. That's what matters.

My Haunted Manor USA

In 2023, our work at the hotel took a significant leap forward when I attended the Festival of the Unexplained. This event is a huge gathering of paranormal investigators and enthusiasts from all over the world, and it was the perfect place to network and share ideas.

While I was there, I met Daryl Marston from the US show 'Ghost Hunters', who was visiting the UK for the first time. Daryl had heard about My Haunted Hotel and was curious to see it for himself. After hearing about what we were doing, he came along to the hotel and even conducted an investigation with British investigators Karen Fray and Rachel Ashman. It was clear from the moment Daryl stepped into the building that he was hooked. He loved the concept and what we were doing with the show.

As soon as he got back to the States, he called me up and said, "I want in on this. I want to bring this to the US." And that's how My Haunted Manor USA was born. What had started as a unique UK-based project was now about to expand across the Atlantic, bringing the My Haunted concept to a whole new audience. It was an incredible moment for us.

Daryl already had a few potential locations in mind when we first discussed expanding the project into the US. He wanted a place with genuine history and a strong paranormal presence, somewhere that would fit the My Haunted ethos of long-term investigation. After looking into several spots, he ultimately chose the Samuel Miller Mansion in Columbia, Pennsylvania. The mansion was steeped in history, with deep ties to the Civil War, Gettysburg, and even the underground railroad. It was the perfect choice, not just for its historical significance but because the paranormal reports from the site were off the charts.

We wasted no time reaching out to the owners, Chris and Amy Raudabaugh, to discuss the possibility of using their location for My Haunted Manor USA. They were intrigued by the idea, and, after a few conversations and negotiations, we struck a deal. It wasn't long after that Harry, Brett, and I were on a plane to the US to set everything up.

Harry had originally come up with the My Haunted Hotel name, but as our conversations about expansion continued, it became clear that the project was outgrowing just one location. We needed something that reflected the scale of what we were building. That's when we rebranded to 'My Haunted Project', allowing for future growth and flexibility. My Haunted Hotel would remain, but naturally became the base for My Haunted HQ, while My Haunted Manor USA would be the first step in expanding internationally.

This structure allowed us to manage both the UK and US locations under the same umbrella, ensuring consistency in the way we approached paranormal investigations while also letting each location maintain its own unique identity. Daryl brought on Jeff and Trey Bader in the US, both of whom shared his passion for the paranormal and immediately fell in love with the format.

The format in the US mirrors exactly what we've established in the UK. Just like at My Haunted Hotel, My Haunted Manor USA operates as an ongoing paranormal investigation where guests stay overnight and their experiences are recorded by a full surveillance system. The Samuel Miller Mansion is equipped with a similar setup to Ye Olde King's Head, with cameras covering every angle and a team on-site monitoring everything that happens throughout the night.

Jeff oversees the camera work and helps coordinate the flow of each episode, making sure all the key moments are captured. Once they have the raw footage, the team sends it over to me, where I take on the full production process. I handle everything from cleaning up the footage to editing and preparing it for release. Our main production office ensures that everything meets the same standards, so whether you're watching content from the UK or the US, the experience and quality are consistent across the board.

The US content has been really well-received by our existing British audience, which has been amazing to see. What's been particularly exciting is that some of our most loyal UK fans, who regularly visit My Haunted Hotel, have even flown over to the US just to investigate at the manor. That level of dedication and interest has been incredible, and it shows just how invested people have become in 'My Haunted Project'.

The international interest continues to grow, and seeing the enthusiasm from both sides of the Atlantic has been a huge boost for us. The fact that the concept resonates so strongly in both the UK and the US is something we're really proud of, and it motivates us to keep pushing the project further.

Now that 'My Haunted Project' is established, and with the Samuel Miller Mansion as our American flagship, the future looks wide open, there's no limit to where we can take this. Our vision is to revolutionise the paranormal scene globally by shifting the focus to long-term, sustained paranormal investigation rooted in a rational, evidence-based approach, moving away from the sensationalist, demon-centric narratives that have dominated paranormal television for years.

Instead of focusing purely on entertainment, we aim to document genuine experiences, whether they end up being debunked or remain unexplained. This shift has the potential to reshape how people engage with the paranormal, showing that credible, methodical investigations are not only more reliable but just as captivating as the flashy, overproduced content people have grown used to. We want to push the field forward, offering viewers something real and authentic.

Unlike many other shows, we make it a point to either debunk the phenomena or acknowledge when something remains unexplained. By paranormal, we mean anything that falls outside the boundaries of normal - something we can't immediately explain. It doesn't necessarily point to ghosts or the supernatural. It's simply an anomaly that warrants further investigation.

We're actively working to expand our portfolio with more locations. One of our top prospects in the UK is

Woolton Hall in Liverpool, a site with incredible history, although it's proving to be a bit of a challenge due to the building's deteriorating condition and local council complications. Woolton Hall was originally built around 1700 for the Molyneux family and has housed several notable figures, including Frederick Richard Leyland, a prominent Liverpool shipowner. During World War II, it served as a hospital, and later it became a meeting place for the Freemasons before transforming into a school. The place is packed with historical significance, and we'd love to bring it under the same continued observation as My Haunted Hotel. However, projects like this take time, and we know it's all part of the journey to uncover the truth behind these fascinating locations.

We're also seriously exploring the possibility of expanding to even more locations across the US, particularly on the west coast of America. If everything falls into place, we could be announcing something major in 2025. This marks only the beginning for 'My Haunted Project'. The project was growing faster than we could have ever anticipated, and it felt like we were only just getting started.

The Future

It's fitting to sum up where things stand now as I reflect on the journey I've laid out in this book. What does the future hold for me? Honestly, I don't know. It's hard to say with certainty, especially in a world and field that's constantly shifting. Earlier this year, I found myself at a real crossroads. I lost my passion for the paranormal entirely. The state of the field, with all its negativity, toxicity, and the rising influence of debunkers and fakers, had left me disillusioned. For the first time in my life, I was seriously considering walking away from everything I'd built. It wasn't just the online drama or the constant attacks, it was the feeling that the paranormal field had become more about egos and entertainment than genuine exploration.

I sat down with Alice, and we had some really tough conversations. I had to reassess everything, look at where I was, what the paranormal meant to me, and where it was all going. But then came a turning point, a much needed holiday to Italy. The trip was a genuine break from work and life in general, it gave me a chance to relax, reflect, and most importantly switch off from social media for week.

It's a paranormal convention that I've always enjoyed, and attending it this year reminded me of why I do this. I got to reconnect with so many good friends and share positive stories, experiences, and that passion we all have for the unknown. It brought me back to the core of why I love this field. Being surrounded by like-minded people, immersed in discussions about the mysteries we're all trying to uncover, helped rekindle the spark I thought I'd lost. It made me realise that the paranormal isn't just about the field itself. It's about the community and the connections we make along the way.

That's when I realised the truth: no matter how much negativity and drama there is, the paranormal bug never really lets go of you. I'd find myself at some historic location, feeling that little buzz, wondering if it's haunted. It's moments like that, far away from the noise and toxicity, that remind me how much I still love this. There's something about stepping into an old building, breathing in its history, and wondering if the walls hold secrets that haven't been uncovered. That curiosity, that drive to understand what might be lingering in the shadows, is what keeps pulling me back in.

Right now, my focus is fully on 'My Haunted Project'. It's become a huge part of my life and something I genuinely believe in. I'm convinced it's going to achieve great things. But I'm busier than ever because of it. I'm working full-time on the project, overseeing the production of 'My Haunted Hotel' and 'My Haunted Manor USA'. It's a lot to juggle, and sometimes I'm working 14-hour days. But it's all worth it.

The dedication to getting everything just right, from the investigations to the production quality, takes a toll, but I wouldn't have it any other way. The excitement of building something that blends real research with engaging content is what keeps me pushing forward. There's a sense that we're on the verge of something bigger, something that could reshape how paranormal investigations are approached, and that makes all the hard work feel like it's leading to something monumental.

Despite my heavy involvement in 'My Haunted Project', I've still found time to take on other projects too. Last Halloween, I worked with Kraken Rum on a paranormal-themed campaign that was creative departure from my usual work and allowed me to explore the lighter, more entertaining side of the paranormal.

Just last year, I filmed with Rylan Clark for a project with Amazon Alexa that hasn't aired yet, which was an interesting experience, blending tech and the paranormal. There's also a pilot I filmed this year with Guz Khan and Lucy Beaumont for a comedy paranormal show for Sky, which was a lot of fun and allowed me to show a different side of myself. These opportunities keep things fresh for me, and I'm always open to taking on new challenges.

One of the more personal projects I managed to squeeze in was an online show on YouTube called 'The Paranormal Investigator'. It's something I produced and devised myself, and it's very close to my heart. This show is a chance for me to investigate locations I'm passionate about, to show people how I approach an investigation, and to share my journey into the paranormal in a way that's deeply personal.

I made it free to watch on YouTube because I wanted to give something back to my fans, who have supported me through thick and thin over the years. The episodes give me full creative control, allowing me to explore locations in more depth than I might in other projects. It's a no-frills, raw look at what real paranormal investigation means to me, and I think that's resonated with viewers who are looking for something more authentic.

The first episode of this new series started with an investigation at Wilderhope Manor, a lesser-known location with a fascinating history dating back to 1585. The Smallman family, who owned it for over 200 years, left behind stories of paranormal activity such as growling sounds, distant voices, and that unmistakable feeling of being watched. It's the kind of place that's not on the usual paranormal radar, which made it even more intriguing to me. I love the idea of exploring locations that haven't been overexposed or sensationalised. It set the tone for the entire series, where I wanted to focus on authentic, overlooked sites and give them the attention they deserve.

Filming the series was a very different experience. It was just me with Alice behind the camera, so it was a lot more relaxed than working with a full team. But it was also deeply serious. I wanted this to be a show where I could take my time, investigate properly, and avoid all the overdramatisation you see in other paranormal series. I wanted to prove that you can make a paranormal show entertaining without falling into that trap.

Throughout the first investigation, both Alice and I felt like we were being followed, and we tried to debunk the noises we heard, but we couldn't find any logical explanation. Fear did creep in at times, but I did my best to stay focused and rational, and I think we succeeded in that.

Looking ahead, there are plans for a second series of the revamped 'The Haunted Hunts' on Amazon Prime, and we've even started bringing back The Haunted Hunts events due to popular demand. While the events aren't as frequent as they once were, we'll still be hosting them here and there for those who want to experience it again.

The events will focus more on the education side of paranormal investigation, giving attendees a chance to learn the methods we've developed over the years. We're taking a more selective approach, choosing locations that truly stand out and offer real potential for activity. It's about quality over quantity now, making sure each event is special and not just another ghost hunt. It feels good to bring them back in this more refined way.

The biggest focus for me right now is definitely 'My Haunted Project'. I'm genuinely passionate about pushing this format forward and maybe even shaping the next generation of paranormal investigators. I've noticed a growing interest in the paranormal from younger people, and I think if we could guide them through the format we've created with 'My Haunted Project', it would be a massive step in the right direction.

Right now, a lot of what's out there on TV and YouTube isn't helping them. It's not showing them what real, long-term paranormal investigation looks like. Most of what they're exposed to is sensationalised and doesn't reflect the patience and methodology needed for serious research. I want to change that to show them that a rational, evidence-based approach is far more rewarding, even if it doesn't produce fireworks in every episode. If I can inspire younger investigators to take this path, I'll feel like I've made a real contribution to the future of the field.

We've got big plans for 'My Haunted Project' going forward. The project itself has been running for two and a half years now. Initially, we thought, "Let's put it on YouTube. It's free, it's accessible, and we can build a fan base from there." That decision allowed us to grow organically, without the pressure of network expectations. YouTube gave us the freedom to do things our way, experiment with the format, and let the audience come to us naturally.

In those two and a half years, we managed to gain 50,000 subscribers, which isn't bad at all. But we soon realised that YouTube wasn't the right platform for what we were doing. 'My Haunted Project' is about an ongoing, long-term investigation. It's not your typical ghost-hunting show where you're at a different location for each episode, and things are wrapped up neatly in 45 minutes.

This is about really getting to grips with a location over time, and that just doesn't work on YouTube. The platform is designed for fast consumption. People want to be hooked within the first 10 seconds, and the type of show we're making simply can't be boiled down to that kind of quick-hit content. YouTube tends to favour flashy, fast-paced videos with dramatic edits, which doesn't align with the more methodical, immersive experience we're aiming for.

I've said it before, but it's important to cover this here in the book: moving from television to YouTube wasn't something I enjoyed. The paranormal scene on YouTube is at an all-time low. It's completely overrun with fake content, sensationalism, and clickbait. The platform rewards this kind of behaviour because the algorithm favours anything that gets quick engagement, whether it's real or not.

Add in the toxic element of debunkers spinning false narratives, and it's just a mess. It doesn't mean all paranormal YouTube channels are bad. There are some great ones like the Ouija Brothers and Ghosts On Trent, who are real supporters of our work and have had great experiences at the hotel, but in general, the scene is not in a good place.

So it became clear to us that YouTube wasn't where 'My Haunted Project' belonged. We needed to get off that platform and move to something more suited to the type of ongoing, investigative content we're making. That's why I'm so excited about the next big step for the project: we're taking 'My Haunted Project' to Amazon Prime. We'll still be putting content out on YouTube, things like behind-the-scenes footage, updates, and little extras for the fans, but when it comes to the main show, Amazon Prime is where it belongs. Amazon offers a more fitting platform, one where audiences are more invested in episodic series and can appreciate the slow-burn, evidence-based approach that 'My Haunted Project' is all about.

The new Amazon Prime show will be called 'My Haunted Project', and it will bring together all of the My Haunted locations under one umbrella. The first series will focus entirely on My Haunted Hotel, taking viewers through the full journey of the hotel. We'll start with the history of Ye Olde King's Head, exploring its centuries-old reputation for paranormal activity, before delving into how the idea for 'My Haunted Hotel' came about. We'll cover everything from the early challenges we faced to the incredible growth we've experienced, and it will culminate in our conclusions about the paranormal activity we've documented over the years.

Series two will then introduce My Haunted Manor USA, where we'll look at how we brought that project to life, the history of the Samuel Miller Mansion, and the experiences the team has had there. If everything goes to plan, season three will introduce a brand-new My

Haunted location, expanding the project even further. The potential for this format is huge. We could keep it going season after season, with each new location offering its own unique history and paranormal mysteries to uncover.

But don't worry. If you come along to the hotel, we're still actively filming. While the new show will have a more documentary-style format, recapping everything that's happened so far, the hotel remains open every week, and we're still documenting the guests' investigations as they unfold. We're not closing the doors just because we've got the Amazon Prime deal in the works.

In fact, anything that happens between now and when we officially start shooting in 2025 could still make it into the show. So, whether you're a returning guest or it's your first time at My Haunted Hotel, you could find yourself part of the next chapter of this incredible journey.

This new chapter for 'My Haunted Project' feels like a huge leap forward, not just for us but for the entire paranormal field. I truly believe that what we're doing has the potential to reshape the way paranormal investigation is presented to the world.

Our focus on long-term research, real eyewitness accounts, and meticulously documented evidence moves away from the tired formula of sensationalism and manufactured drama. Instead, we're bringing something genuine, something that I hope will inspire future generations of investigators.

If this approach becomes the norm, then maybe we'll finally start to get closer to understanding what's really out there. This is what I believe the future of the paranormal should look like, and it's just the beginning.

Printed in Great Britain
by Amazon